LIFE'S A ROLLERCOASTER, I'M JUST HERE FOR THE RIDE

Nia Fenix

FENIX RISING PRESS

This book is rooted in lived experience, reflection, and research. Some names and identifying details may have been changed to protect privacy.

Published by Fenix Rising Press
An imprint of Fenix Creative Works
https://fenixcreativeworks.com/

First edition, 2026

ISBN (paperback): 979-8-9947065-0-3
ISBN (ebook): 979-8-9947065-1-0

Cover design Fenix Creative Works

Printed in the United States of America

CONTENTS

DEDICATION

To everyone walking through their own storm — may you always find the laughter in the chaos, the light in the cracks, and the strength in yourself... even on the days you feel like a soggy sock.

And to my people — the ones who never flinched when things got weird, messy, or dramatically overshared; who endured my temper tantrums, played charades on my speechless days, and showed up without hesitation. You saw me through it all, and you keep showing up anyway — that's love.

This book is for all of you!

Disclaimer (a.k.a. The "Please Don't Sue Me" Section)

B efore we dive into this beautifully chaotic, painfully honest, and hopefully hilarious journey, let me just say this: I am not a doctor, therapist, or certified anything except a professional human who's lived through some stuff.

This book is based on my personal experiences, reflections, and hard-earned lessons – served with a side of humor and a sprinkle of sass. While I talk a lot about health, grief, mental wellness, and self-care, none of this is intended to be medical advice. Seriously. If something I share resonates with you – amazing. If something feels

LIFE'S A ROLLERCOASTER, I'M...

off – please trust your gut, and talk to a qualified health-care or mental health professional.

Translation: I can't diagnose you, treat you, or prescribe you anything... except maybe a laugh or two and a reminder that you're not alone. *You* are the expert of your own life. Take what helps, leave what doesn't, and always, *always* prioritize your well-being.

WELCOME TO THE ROLLERCOASTER!

PLEASE KEEP YOUR ARMS AND LEGS INSIDE THE RIDE

Welcome to my story!

Buckle up, because we're about to dive into a journey that's anything but ordinary. What started as the usual hustle and bustle of life quickly morphed into a chaotic whirlwind of health issues, doctor's appointments, and more tests than I ever thought were humanly possible. For years, I played detective, searching for answers like a health mystery novel with way too many plot twists. And let's just say: this wasn't the kind of roller coaster you sign up for on vacation. But here I am, writing this book, because the crazy ride turned out to be far more than just a struggle — it was a transformation.

Now, don't worry — this isn't going to be a dry medical journal. Yes, the first section of the book digs into my health journey, but it's all about the wild ride of figuring out what happened to my body (spoiler: still figuring it out). I believe that understanding where I've been — all the blood tests, diagnosis mysteries, and moments of sheer disbelief — will give you a deeper appreciation for the heart of the story, which really kicks off in Section 2: "*Adjust, Adapt, Amaze: The Art of Rolling With It*". In this section, we're going deep into the art of resilience, humor, and figuring out how to live life with a totally new set of rules when everything you thought was "normal" gets tossed out the window.

And let's be real: the things I share in Section 2? They aren't groundbreaking, never-before-heard secrets. You've probably heard them all before. (Self-love! Adaptation! Perception! Humor!) But knowing and *doing* are two very different beasts. It's one thing to know you should be kind to yourself. It's another to actually practice it when life is serving you a hot mess with a side of WTH.

That's why I invite you — no, lovingly *dare* you — to give each chapter in Section 2 a good solid 2-3 days of intentional effort. Try the practices. Sit with the ideas. Be mindful of what shifts, even just a little, in your thoughts or emotions. Consider it a mini challenge from me to you. No pressure — just curiosity. Because the beauty of change lies not in grand gestures, but in tiny, consistent nudges.

And let me tell you, this book is about to take you on a full-spectrum emotional rollercoaster. One minute, you'll be laughing so hard you snort (I take zero responsibility for any beverages that end up in your sinuses), and the next, you might be wiping away a tear (or ten). I'm talking highs, lows, and every awkward, weird, and messy middle moment. You'll experience the range — from the frustration of not being heard by doctors to the joy of finding new ways to adapt when everything feels out of control. You'll see the vulnerable moments where I've had to dig deep and learn to love myself when it felt the hardest. But you'll also see the funny side of life — because if you can't laugh at your own chaos, you might just go a little crazy.

This book isn't just about me and my health challenges — it's about how we all go through tough times and come out stronger on the other side. Whether you're facing your own storm, helping someone you care about navigate theirs, or simply wanted to come along for the ride, I hope you find something in these pages that resonates with you. Maybe it's the reminder that you're not alone, or the knowledge that it's okay to stumble, cry, laugh, and celebrate all at once. Whatever it is, I want you to know that this book is here for you, just as much as it's been a lifeline for me to write.

So, get ready. This ride isn't smooth sailing. It's messy, imperfect, and full of curveballs, but it's also full of love, humor, and a whole lot of growth. You're going to laugh, cry, and maybe even shout "What the heck?!" at some point — but trust me, it's all part of the adventure.

So... are you ready? let's do this. Let's visit the full spectrum of emotions together. And remember: if nothing else, at least we'll have a few laughs along the way.

Strap on your seatbelts, make sure they're secure, and please remember to keep your arms and legs inside the ride at all times for your own safety.

Section 1: Adventures in Malfunction - A Body's Greatest Hits

Before I Became the Main Character in a Medical Drama

Deciding where to start this story was no easy task. My life has been anything but boring, and if I were to recount every detail from the beginning, we might as well publish it as a series of encyclopedias. Let's skip the encyclopedia-sized version, shall we?

My childhood was a pretty good one, surrounded by a family that showered me with love and support. But being the stubborn, headstrong kid I was, I often let my invincibility complex (yes, I have one of those) get the better of me. Let's just say I learned a lot of life lessons the hard way, and my list of "what not to do" grew exponentially. Friendships came and went like the changing tides, some leaving lasting imprints, others fading like footprints in the sand.

Motherhood, despite its shortness in my case, was an experience that gifted me with immeasurable joy, unique challenges, and a deep sense of fulfillment. The memories I made are treasures I hold close to my heart. Though I wasn't fully prepared for the journey (are we ever?), I navigated it the best I could with the tools I had at the time.

Like many, I look back with a touch of longing, wishing I could have done more. It's just another item on that ever-growing list of life's "coulda, woulda, shoulda's". If only we had a crystal ball to guide us, right? But alas, such is the bittersweet nature of life's journey. As the saying goes, *"Life is like a box of chocolates - you never know what you're gonna get!"* (Props to Forrest Gump!)

Like any good rollercoaster, my life's journey comes with its share of climbing heights, unexpected dips, and sharp turns. I've taken wrong paths, stumbled over my own feet, and yes, even face-planted more times than I'd like to admit. Mistakes were made, bridges burned, and more than a few "what was I thinking?!" moments are etched into my personal history.

But those blunders, those cringe-worthy missteps, those epic fails? They've been my most valuable teachers, molding me into the imperfect, beautifully flawed human I am today. I wouldn't trade those experiences for anything, for they've taught me more about resilience, forgiveness, and the power of second (or third, or tenth) chances than any textbook ever could.

Throughout my life, I've always strived to be a beacon of positivity, radiating optimism and a natural inclination to assist others. It's just in my DNA - extending a helping hand, sprinkling a little sunshine, and injecting some fun into every situation! I thrive on making people chuckle and flipping frowns into smiles.

My career in customer service was a perfect fit, as I excelled at forging connections with individuals and turning challenging scenarios into success stories. I became known for my compassionate and empathetic nature, my quirky sense of humor, and my boundless energy - always eager to lend a hand. I made a conscious effort to savor life's moments, big and small, and to pause and appreciate the beauty around me.

In a nutshell, I'm the kind of person who not only stops to smell the flowers, but also stops to crack a joke and spread some joy. Life's too short to be anything but witty and wonderful! Now, that's not to say I'm always a walking ray of sunshine. I have my moments—stubborn as a mule, expecting too much, occasionally throwing myself a first-class pity party. But at the end of the day, I do my best to shake it off, find solutions instead of dwelling on problems, and, most importantly, keep laughing through it all.

My life may have had a few more curve balls than most, but hey, who's keeping score anyway? Comparing struggles is like comparing apples and oranges - everyone faces their own unique challenges, but everyone has them. Just because someone else's journey looks different doesn't diminish the weight of your own battles. But more on that later.

Alright, folks, enough with the pre-show chatter. It's time to fasten your seatbelts and brace yourselves, because the main event is about to begin.

We're diving headfirst into the year 2020, where the plot truly thickens. But before we do, a quick disclaimer: my memory isn't what it used to be, thanks to the delightful quirks of my brain. So, while I'll do my best to recount the events as accurately as possible, please bear with me if a few details get a little fuzzy.

This is my story, to the best of my recollection.

2020

Earning my psychology degree was anything but a straight shot—it was more like a scenic route filled with detours, potholes, and the occasional "*Are we there yet?*" moment. But after nearly a decade of perseverance (because, of course, I'd turn a four-year degree into a ten-year saga), I finally crossed the finish line at the end of 2019, diploma in hand. Cue the confetti! VICTORY AT LAST!

Then came the infamous COVID lockdown. Are you kidding me?!? I finally cross the finish line, diploma in hand, ready to conquer the world... and *boom*—I'm under house arrest. Figures. Like everyone else, I was climbing the walls, bursting with pent-up energy and ambition. Armed with my freshly minted degree and a head full of big dreams, I was all set to make a difference. Instead, my biggest accomplishment was perfecting the art of changing from night pajamas to day pajamas.

When the lockdown finally ended, I was more than ready for a fresh start. So, with a suitcase full of hope and a degree practically begging to be used, I packed my bags and moved to a new state, eager to dive headfirst into the world of psychology.

The first year of the move was fantastic! Every morning (unless it was raining or colder than my motivation on a Monday), I faithfully walked two-plus miles on the beach, soaking in a full five-sensory recharge as the sun rose. Then, I'd dive into 10-12 hours at a temporary job while hunting for my grand entrance into the psychology field.

But, as luck would have it, the Universe took one look at my plans, chuckled, and said, *"Yeah... nope."*

Cancer Chaos

Because my mother was diagnosed with—and lost her battle to—breast cancer at a young age, I've always been pretty diligent about doing self-exams. I had a scare once when I found a lump, but thankfully, it turned out to be a false alarm. *Crisis averted!* But, when I found another one, my inner alarm bells went off like a fire drill.

I called my doctor faster than I grab snacks during a commercial break, and they scheduled me for a mammogram. The doctor didn't seem too worried and casually set me up for a follow-up in six months. Cool, cool. No stress.

Fast forward to that follow-up—turns out, the lump had grown. *Cue the dramatic music.* Suddenly, things got real, and they decided to do a biopsy right then and there.

September, 2021—D-Day. My follow-up appointment to go over the biopsy results. I walked in hoping for reassurance, but instead, I got hit with the dreaded "C" word: *cancer*. Breast cancer. My initial reaction? *"I'm sorry, WHAT?!? Breast cancer?!? I'm only 40! Are you sure? Check again. Maybe switch it off and back on?"* At 40 years young, cancer felt completely out of place, like a plot twist in someone else's story—not mine. Surely, there had been a mistake. A mix-up in the paperwork. A cosmic clerical error. Denial hit first. Then came the anger. The sadness. The overwhelming *"Why me?"* I didn't want to believe it. I didn't want to tell anyone. It was like getting sucker-punched by the universe, leaving me breathless and scrambling to make sense of it.

After the diagnosis, everything seemed to go into hyper-speed... FAST. In October, I had a lumpectomy to remove the tumor, along with three lymph nodes for testing (a sentinel lymph node biopsy, or SLNB). One of those three tested positive, so I had to go back for more—an axillary lymph node dissection (ALND), where they removed even more for testing. The verdict? Triple positive breast cancer (ER+, PR+, HER2+) and node positive. The recommended game plan? Six rounds of chemo, 15 rounds of radiation, and medication for 5-10 years.

I was *really* worried. *How am I going to pay for all these treatments? What if I can't work? How will I pay my bills? What if I'm not physically able to take care of myself?* And on and on it went, like a never-ending mental hamster wheel. Anyone who knows me knows that I'm fiercely independent. Asking for help? Not my thing. I'd rather pull a 12-hour workday, handle everything on my own, and *never* sit down. TV? Movies? Please—I'm too busy checking off my to-do list!

After indulging in a solid round of *"Why me?"*, *"This isn't fair!"*, and the ever-classic *"Are you freaking kidding me?!"*, I gave myself a brief mourning period for my derailed plans and shattered expectations. Then, I took a deep breath, dusted off my fighting spirit, and declared, *"Alright,—GAME ON."*

Here's a glimpse of my journal from that time:

> *"The lumpectomy wasn't terrible, all things considered. It wasn't exactly a walk in the park, especially due to the location, but it was manageable. The area where the lymph nodes were removed, though? Totally different story. The lymph nodes are taken*

from under my arm, in the armpit area. I decided to skip the drain, so I was stuck changing gauze and bandages all. the. time. OOWW. I had swelling in my arm, along with shooting pains, numbness, and tingling. The doctor warned me this could last anywhere from a few weeks to a few years... or even a lifetime. Great. I've been doing the recommended exercises to prevent losing motion in my arm and shoulder, but it's a slow road."

"It's been a month since the ALND. The swelling has mostly gone down, but the shooting pains and tingling are still going strong. At least the arm compression sleeve helps a bit. Here's the thing I wasn't prepared for, though: sometimes I can't grip things properly. I've broken a few items, spilled countless others, and honestly, I've had more than one meltdown from the sheer frustration of it all. But hey, as they say, "don't cry over spilled milk." So, I remind

myself this won't last forever. It's all one day at a time..."

It was tough, but I knew I had to keep pushing forward—one day at a time.

My recommended chemo treatment was a "drug cocktail" called TCHP, which consists of four drugs: Docetaxel (Taxotere), Carboplatin (Paraplatin), Trastuzumab (Herceptin), and Pertuzumab (Perjeta). They'd administer all four drugs on treatment days, every 21 days—those 21 days are referred to as a "cycle".

Naturally, being me, I had a ton of questions. What exactly are these drugs? What side effects should I expect? From what I gathered, in simple terms, these drugs target cancer cells to either kill them or slow their growth. The potential side effects seemed endless, but the main ones? Nausea, diarrhea or constipation, hair loss, fatigue, anemia, and low white blood cell counts. I asked a lot of questions and did tons of research on my own. Admittedly, I may have gone a little overboard and potentially scared myself more with the info I found—but I needed to *know*. Prepare for the worst, hope for the best, right?

One thing I discovered through my research (and conversations with people who'd already been through chemo) was that when your hair falls out due to chemo, it doesn't just thin gradually. No, it falls out in clumps. When I first read that, my mind immediately flashed to an image of me brushing my hair and a massive clump coming out. I knew I'd completely lose it if that happened. So, before my first chemo, I made the decision to shave my head. Yes, it was hard, and yes, I cried like a baby. But I chose the less traumatic option for *me*.

My first chemo was scheduled for November. The doctor told me to expect the first treatment to be an all-day affair—6-8 hours, depending on how my body responded. As the days crept closer, my anxiety grew. How would my body react? What side effects would I experience? How long would they last? I wouldn't have to wonder for long... I was about to find out!

Chemo was a wild ride. It became my constant unwelcome companion, round after relentless round. The initial treatments were uncomfortable, sure, but manageable. However, as the weeks dragged on, chemo seemed to take on a life of its own, wreaking havoc on my body. Nausea and vomiting became relentless, making it nearly impossible to keep anything down. Dizziness swirled around me like a never-ending teacup ride, and a migraine clamped down on my skull, rendering me helpless and immobile. Fainting spells became part of my routine, adding chaos to my already tumultuous existence. To top it off, unpredictable mood swings and emotional outbursts turned my reflection into a stranger. Who was this person, with their volatile emotions and uncharacteristic reactions? It was disorienting and completely unsettling.

As the chemo took its toll, I found myself pushed to the brink. With each round, the side effects grew more severe, casting a shadow over my daily life. The doctors kept reassuring me that the symptoms were temporary, just part of the treatment. But it felt like I was losing control of myself while fighting a life-threatening illness. Finally, I reached a turning point. I realized continuing chemo wasn't sustainable. In a moment of clarity, I made the decision to stop and agreed to additional radiation therapy instead. And while that decision brought its own challenges, it was a step toward reclaiming some control over my body and my life.

The transition from chemo to radiation was akin to trading a hurricane for a thunderstorm. While not exactly enjoyable, radiation was far more tolerable. Sure, I did end up with some pretty severe burns toward the end, even though I was ridiculously diligent about slathering on aloe and all sorts of soothing lotions multiple times a day. It wasn't exactly a walk in the park, but it definitely wasn't the nightmare that chemo was! I was so eager to complete my treatment that I marked each session by gleefully popping a balloon from a colorful chain I'd created.

By the summer of 2022, I had finally crossed the finish line of cancer treatment, and let me tell you, it felt like pure euphoria. I was over the moon, practically doing cartwheels in my mind (though my body wasn't quite ready for the real thing yet—let's just say my coordination was still recovering from chemo). Sure, there were some lingering symptoms, but I was deemed cancer free (WHOO HOO!), the brutal treatments were finally behind me, and I figured the symptoms would soon fade, and I'd gradually ease back into my "normal" self. I was all set to reclaim my life, dust off those long-forgotten goals, and hit the ground running.

Or so I thought...

THE EYE OF THE STORM

Are you familiar with a hurricane and the "eye of the storm"? That brief, eerie calm before the storm slams back in full force? Well, from the hazy summer of 2022, when I wrapped up the cancer treatment, until around February 2023, it felt like my eye of the storm. It was quiet, almost surreal, as I started emerging from the fog of illness like a phoenix—minus the fiery explosions, of course. Slowly but surely, I got stronger and more determined.

By the end of 2022, I had returned to work, easing in with just a few hours a week and building up my stamina like a slow, but steady, tortoise on a mission. Cooking, walking, and even laughing felt like winning the lottery, each moment a tiny victory. But no matter how much I celebrated, the lingering symptoms were like that uninvited guest who refuses to leave, always reminding me of the tough battle I'd fought and the strength it took to get here.

By the end of 2022, I was down to just 1–3 "bad days" a month—nausea, vomiting, and the occasional impromptu nap (a.k.a. fainting spell) still lurking as unwelcome reminders that my recovery wasn't quite done with me. But in February 2023, those bad days started creeping back in, like an ex I never wanted to see again.

My customer service job became a daily test of endurance, as I struggled to keep my composure while battling the unpredictable symptoms. It wasn't unusual for me to vanish mid-conversation with a client, only to return moments later, disoriented and apologizing. Let's just say being a "frequent fainter" isn't the best asset in customer service.

Naturally, I turned to the medical community for answers, hoping for a lifeline in the storm. The doctors, in their infinite wisdom, chalked the symptoms up to lingering chemo side effects. After my primary doctor referred me to a neurologist in January, I was stunned to find that the earliest appointment available wasn't until June. So, in the meantime, I had to navigate the unpredictable waters of my new reality. It was like walking a tightrope—juggling daily life while my body did its best to keep me on my toes. Despite it all, I held onto the hope that one day, my symptoms would vanish into thin air.

And then...

And then begins the next chapter in the story—one I never saw coming, but one that would test me in ways I never imagined.

ABS-solutely Not What I Ordered

Note: ABS and FND were happening simultaneously, but for clarity, I've separated them in this book to avoid confusion between the two disorders.

So, after surviving the hell of chemo and radiation, earning my hard-fought title as a breast cancer survivor in remission, and finally feeling like I was reclaiming my old self—*BOOM*! My body pulled a plot twist. The symptoms reappeared like a villain in a horror movie, dramatically announcing, *"Miss me?"*

Spring 2023 didn't just arrive—it came in swinging, and not in a fun, beachy "spring break" kind of way.

The bad days returned with a vengeance, turning up the intensity until they completely hijacked my life. Nausea, vomiting, migraines, and fainting spells (plus the bonus bruises from my impromptu floor meetings) became my unwelcome daily routine. My so-called "recovery" felt like the universe's cruel joke... but I was definitely NOT laughing. By the time March ended, my symptoms had officially moved in, unpacked their bags, and showed no signs of leaving.

April 17th—a date permanently stamped into my memory as the day my body pulled its most dramatic stunt yet. After days of radio silence, my loved ones found me unconscious on the floor, my body once again proving it had a mind of its own. The officer's chilling words, *"dead on arrival,"* set the tone as I was rushed to the hospital. When I finally woke up, everything was a foggy mess of confusion. *What day was it? How long had I been out? What happened*? Just another day in my medical mystery saga, right?

The ER visit? Oh, *that* was a fun ride. Aside from my blood pressure casually soaring to 183/104 (totally normal, I'm sure), all my tests came back perfectly fine— except for one *tiny* detail: a blood alcohol level of 200. *Excuse me?!?* I don't drink. I already have enough nausea, dizziness, and general chaos in my life without adding tequila to the mix. And yet, somehow, my blood work suggested I should be three sheets to the wind—except I was sitting there, talking normally, without a single slur. At 100 pounds, that level should have had me comatose... or worse.

Was this some kind of prank? Were hidden cameras about to pop out? Because if so, it was *not* funny. Was I hallucinating? Had my meds finally pushed me into full-blown madness? What was happening?!

The attending physician, radiating pure smugness, confidently declared that I was just another drunken mess. My protests? Ignored. My insistence that I hadn't touched a drop of alcohol? Brushed off like yesterday's news. According to him, my sky-high blood alcohol level was the obvious culprit—never mind the whole I don't drink thing. Apparently, I was a closet drunk, and he was *determined* to prove it. The condescending cherry on top? His official notes from the visit:

> *"Patient's alcohol level is 200. Patient denies drinking. When I told patient this in front of others in the room, she became very angry, stating that she does not drink. I offered*

privacy to patient; however, she did not want people to leave the room."

Ah, yes. Because clearly, the *real* issue wasn't my mysterious symptoms or the medical anomaly staring him in the face—it was my so-called *attitude*.

My memory of the incident—and the days leading up to it—were a blur, but one thing I knew for sure: I wasn't a secret drinker. Yet, after exhausting myself by adamantly denying it and the doctor just as adamantly insisting otherwise, I suddenly became the *problem patient* who *"wanted to leave against medical advice."*

His official diagnosis? *"Altered mental status due to alcohol intoxication."* His expert medical advice? *"Just stop drinking."*

Oh, of course! How had I not thought of that? Never mind my long history of fainting spells or the fact that I was *sober*—those pesky details didn't seem to matter. It was a losing battle against arrogance and assumptions, and I walked out of that ER feeling frustrated, dismissed, and no closer to understanding what was actually happening to my body.

I knew without a doubt that I hadn't been drinking—so if the doctors weren't going to take me seriously,

I'd just have to take matters into my own hands. Fueled by frustration (and a healthy dose of stubbornness), I dove headfirst into internet research, determined to crack the case myself.

That's when I stumbled upon auto-brewery syndrome (ABS)—a rare and bizarre condition where the gut ferments carbohydrates and sugars into alcohol. Basically, my body could be running its own personal brewery... without my consent. It sounded ridiculous, but at this point, so did everything else. Could this be the missing puzzle piece?

Of course, since ABS is so rare, finding a doctor who actually knew about it—let alone believed in it—was going to be a whole new battle. But hey, I had fought tougher fights before.

Two weeks later, after enduring more symptoms and getting the cold shoulder from multiple urgent care centers, a friend came to my rescue. They drove me two and a half hours to another hospital that is considered one of the best in the state, determined to find some answers. More tests were done, but of course, they all came back normal. The diagnosis? Catatonia—an extreme state of immobility and unresponsiveness, where the mind and body seem to shut down. No one could tell me why I was in this state, just that I was. It felt like a punch to the gut, as though I was being told, *"We have no clue, but we're giving it a name."*

Frustrating doesn't even begin to cover it. I left that hospital with even more questions than when I arrived—no concrete answers, no real explanation for my bizarre symptoms, and nothing to hold onto. But amidst all the confusion, there was a tiny spark of hope: I was referred to both neurology and cardiology at this far-off hospital. And shockingly, neurology had an opening in May. A whole month away, but still—it was something. I marked the date on my calendar, half excited and half terrified about what I might find out.

The relentless symptoms continued their assault on my body, and now I was dealing with a whole new level of horror: blood in both my stool and vomit, showing up regularly. It felt like my body had turned against me completely. Desperate for answers, I took the doctor's advice and headed to a smaller, nearby hospital, hoping that in their quieter setting, my concerns might be taken more seriously. The doctor even wrote a letter of recommendation for me to get some imaging on my stomach, a small act that actually sparked a flicker of hope in an otherwise dismal situation. Maybe this time, things would be different.

Unfortunately, that glimmer of hope was quickly snuffed out. With limited resources, the smaller facility couldn't offer the comprehensive care I needed, and once again, I was referred back to the main hospital. Feeling a sense of déjà vu, I trudged back to the same sterile hallways and skeptical stares. Spoiler alert: if I thought my last hospital visit was frustrating, this one would raise the bar for sheer exasperation.

When I arrived at the hospital, I was out cold, so the doctor decided to try increasingly painful methods to rouse me. Yep, painful stimuli as the go-to move. If you're not familiar with the concept (lucky you), it basically involves applying pressure to specific areas of the body to provoke a pain response. And let me tell you—it's *not* fun. After a few attempts, the doctor resorted to a sternum rub. (Ouch!) It finally got me to stir... for about a minute, before I slipped back into unconsciousness. Great timing, right?

During the visit, I told the doctor my genuine fear—I was vomiting and passing blood, and it felt like my body was shutting down. His response? A casual chuckle and a dismissive, *"That's not what the tests show."* As if that magically made the blood disappear. And the note from the other doctor requesting imaging? That got a laugh too, followed by a smug, *"That's not how it works."* Ah, medical gaslighting at its finest!

When I brought up auto-brewery syndrome and how it could explain my bizarre blood alcohol levels, the doctor's response was equal parts amusing and infuriating. He openly admitted to Googling it—yes, *Googling* it—then attempted a makeshift test based on whatever he skimmed from the internet. Points for effort, I guess?

But the real kicker was when he searched my friend's purse, even cracking open her water bottle for a sniff, as if we were running some kind of underground speakeasy. It was surreal, humiliating, and completely ridiculous. On the bright side, he did at least send me home with a prescription to help with the stomach bleeding (that he said was nonexistent)—so... baby steps?

To add insult to injury, here's a glimpse into the doctor's actual notes from that visit: *"I believe this is behavioral... I caught the patient in a lie on arrival – I thought I smelled alcohol... she denies drinking, yet I see she was here previously and she had a BAL of 200."* He went on to belittle the referral letter from the doctor and accused me of faking my symptoms. Apparently, my genuine fear of dying was just a dramatic performance for his amusement. His final conclusion? *"Substance abuse is likely the cause... I think she is having a conversion disorder as well"* (more on this later). In other words, in his mind (and according to his notes), I was making it all up. Not only was I and my concerns dismissed, but I was also accused of being a liar and an addict. It was a devastating blow to my already fragile state.

Yet, two days later, I found myself back in a hospital bed, this time at a different facility. The doctor's bedside manner was a welcome change, offering a glimmer of compassion and empathy that had been sorely lacking in previous encounters. However, despite their best efforts, the elusive answers I sought remained out of reach.

Then came the grand gastroenterology adventure—a colonoscopy and endoscopy to investigate the bloody vomit, nausea, and general stomach rebellion. The findings? *"Diverticulosis and differential diagnoses of infection, medication-induced injury, and active phase of Crohn's disease."* A fancy way of saying... *Nothing that is concerning.* Seriously?

Spring 2023 was a never-ending carousel of medical visits—ER trips, urgent care stops, specialist consultations—yet I was no closer to answers. Despite my desperate pleas, I was either dismissed outright or branded with the ever-popular "secret alcoholic" label. I was so desperate for help that I actually begged to be admitted to the hospital—something no sane person would normally request, but at this point, sanity was a luxury I couldn't afford.

I was blacking out multiple times a day, my stomach was waging war against me, and I was losing blood from both ends like some kind of horror movie special effect. Eating was a joke, keeping food down was even funnier, and my body was running on fumes. And yet, no matter how severe my symptoms became, every doctor seemed to hand me the same lazy, one-size-fits-all diagnosis: *"Just stop drinking, and you'll be fine."* Right... if only it was that easy.

Surprisingly, I eventually finally found a doctor who was actually familiar with Auto-Brewery Syndrome that was within traveling distance—turns out, a family member of hers had it. She ran the necessary tests, and at long last, I had confirmation: I *did* have ABS. *Finally*! Someone who didn't think I was just a closet drunk! FI-NALLY! I had actual medical proof! You *cannot* imagine my relief. I almost wanted to frame the results!

Naturally, my first request was for her to send official documentation to the local hospital, just so it would be on record that I had ABS—and, in fact, *was not* secretly chugging vodka in dark alleys or in my closet at home.

With a solid diagnosis in hand, I kicked off treatment like a champ — armed with medication, probiotics, and a brand-new diet plan that basically screamed *"No fun allowed!"* Sugar? Absolutely not. Carbs? Dream on. Cutting out sugar *and* carbs at the same time? Now *that's* the kind of challenge that deserves a reality show!

But, after about a month, I couldn't argue with the results. I actually started feeling better! Of course, that didn't stop me from occasionally convincing myself that *"just a bite"* wouldn't hurt. Spoiler alert: it did. Turns out, my body wasn't a fan of my little rebellion, and it was quick to remind me who's boss.

The toughest part wasn't just resisting the siren call of sweets and bread — though let's be real, passing by a bakery felt like walking through a house of horrors. It was the food monotony that really got me. Finding things to eat without spiraling into complete boredom became my full-time hobby. And don't even get me started on the joy of watching others indulge, their faces lighting up with that *"Oh my gosh, this is amazing!"* expression. Meanwhile, I sat there with my lettuce and dreams, nodding along like, *"Yay, good for you."*

About a year and a half after my diagnosis, I had become quite the amateur detective, constantly researching, learning, and connecting with others who shared my condition. That's when I stumbled upon a supplement regimen commonly used in Brazil to treat it — we're talking vitamins, minerals, amino acids, and all sorts of "good for you" stuff. Naturally, I ran it by my doctor, who took one look at the list and exclaimed, *"WOW! That's a lot!"* But, with a shrug and a smile, she gave me the green light. Her advice? *"Go for it!"*

And boy, did I go for it. During the glorious "detox phase," I found myself wrangling 13 different bottles of supplements like a pharmacist's worst nightmare. My countertop looked like a science experiment gone rogue. At first, I got a little too enthusiastic and tried taking a bunch of them all at once. Spoiler alert: that didn't go well. Lesson learned! I scaled back and took the slow-and-steady route, introducing a few at a time, letting my body adjust, and then adding a couple more until I was a certified supplement-taking machine.

Then, months later, came the moment of truth — my first experiment. I, the brave soul, decided to dabble in the world of forbidden foods. First up: a small scoop of homemade mashed potatoes. Cue the dramatic dru mroll... *No sickness!* A couple of days later, I went rogue again — this time with a little sugar. *Still no sickness!* Was this real life? Did I just cure myself? I half expected a parade to burst through my front door with confetti and a marching band. Turns out, sometimes the light at the end of the tunnel is just a potato.

Living with ABS has been nothing short of an adventure — like one of those roller coasters you didn't *exactly* sign up for. After three years of navigating the special diet, countless days of throwing up, and eventually figuring out how to manage it, you'd think the battle would be over. Heck, it's even neatly documented in my medical records, stamped and official. But somehow, I still run into doctors who confidently declare, *"That's not a real disorder. It's just a theory."* Oh really? Tell that to my trash can that saw more of my lunches than I did!

The bulk of the medical world has never even *heard* of ABS. And while I'm always happy to throw on my imaginary lab coat and give a quick *"ABS 101"* lesson, I've found most doctors aren't exactly eager to enroll. Call me Professor ABS — now, where's my honorary degree?

As for my so-called "cure," I'm honestly not sure. I can indulge in carbs and sugars now, but I'm no reckless rebel. I'm not out here double-fisting donuts or diving headfirst into a vat of mac 'n' cheese. Partly because I'm not entirely convinced it won't backfire, and partly because — surprise! — after all that time without sugar, some things just don't taste the same. It's like my taste buds took an early retirement.

So, one mystery solved. But what about everything else? Did treating the ABS magically fix all my other delightful symptoms? Nope. Not even close. Apparently, my body missed the memo on "happily ever after." *Sigh.*

Nothing can ever be easy, can it?

MALFUNCTION JUNCTION

MY BRAIN TOOK A DETOUR

While navigating the wild twists and turns of my auto-brewery syndrome adventure, life, of course, decided I needed an encore. Because why settle for one baffling medical mystery when you can have *two*?

As I was meticulously counting carbs and dodging sugar like it was my sworn enemy, my body was busy throwing in a whole new set of challenges. Enter Functional Neurological Disorder — or FND — the plot twist I never saw coming. Now, to keep things a little less chaotic (because trust me, my body already had that covered), I've separated the stories here. But in reality? They were playing out at the same time, making sure I never got too comfortable. So, buckle up — it's time for round two of my body's "Greatest Hits."

Finally, a glimmer of hope appeared in late May 2023—I had my first real appointment with a neurologist away from the chaotic guessing games of the ER. I arrived armed with a painstakingly detailed medical history and a highlight reel of my fainting episodes (courtesy of my ever-vigilant friends). Surely, with actual evidence in hand, I'd finally get some concrete answers.

After reviewing my case, the neurologist hit me with a diagnosis I hadn't seen coming: *"The episodes shown do not have the appearance of classical seizures and instead look more consistent with non-epileptic behavioral spells (PNES)"* (yep, straight from the doctor's notes). We then ventured into the murky world of Functional Neurological Disorder (FND), where the brain and body decide to completely ignore logic. The doctor explained that these disorders could develop as a maladaptive response to chronic pain, stress, or past trauma, causing involuntary movements, non-epileptic seizures, and other symptoms that mimic other neurological conditions.

This all sounded intriguing—except for one glaring issue: *why now*? I had spent my life handling stress, rolling with every punch thrown my way. So why was my body suddenly pulling the emergency brake? Was this some kind of delayed meltdown? A stress tantrum years in the making? The logic didn't add up to me, and neither did my symptoms.

You can imagine my sheer joy (heavy on the sarcasm) when I was handed a couple of websites about FND, told to keep up with psychological therapy (which I had already been in), and then swiftly shown the door. He emphasized that cognitive behavioral therapy (CBT) was the golden ticket to curing me, suggesting it as the most effective treatment for my symptoms. In his notes, he referred to my symptoms as "behavioral," which sounded more like a lecture than a diagnosis. BUT he wanted to rule out other things, just to be sure.

To rule out epilepsy, I was sent for a 72-hour ambulatory EEG, which meant I got to wear a high-tech head-gear setup at home for three days which would record my brain activity. My friends and I diligently recorded each fainting episode by pressing the tracking button—and considering I was having multiple episodes daily, we racked up plenty of data. And yet, despite all that effort, only seven of those recordings were actually reviewed. The results? *"The record shows a good organization at rest, consisting of a 9-10 Hz, 10-30 uV posterior dominant rhythm with good reactivity. There is a moderate bilateral beta activity."* **Translation**: *Everything looked normal.*

Next up, cardiology! I wore a heart monitor for two weeks, tracking every blackout and weird spell. I had an echocardiogram done which showed *"low end of normal valve functioning,"* specifically *"the left ventricle showed mildly decreased functioning"* and *"mild trileaflet regurgitation"* but neither were concerning, and everything else appeared fine. I wore a second heart monitor (about a year later), and this time, rather than push the button (to mark episodes) every episode I had, I only pushed the button to mark incidents when I felt my heart acting funny (beating slowly, skipping beats, etc.). The results of this were slightly different - my heart beat dropped below the norm several times and raised above 115 BPM a few times (mind you, I'm unable to exercise, so there's no reason my heart rate should be that high!). But it wasn't consistent enough to be concerning.

So, all in all, the cardiology results? *Everything looked normal.* (Anyone else sensing a pattern?)

And for the grand finale, I had an MRI. The results? You guessed it—*Everything. Looked. Normal.* At this point, I was starting to wonder if *I* was normal—because nothing about my daily experience screamed "normal" to me!

In June, I finally had my long-awaited appointment with the local neurologist—the one I'd been referred to all the way back in January. Given that he worked with the same hospital where I'd had such stellar experiences, I wasn't exactly brimming with optimism. Spoiler alert: my low expectations were still too high.

He introduced himself as a headache specialist (which was technically relevant, considering my migraines, but hardly the most pressing issue). He then proceeded to conduct what I can only describe as the most half-hearted neurological exam in history. He asked me to squeeze his hands—never mind that my left arm was visibly braced from a fall due to an episode. He had me walk across the room—ignoring the fact that I was limping from a bruised hip from the same fall.

Instead of inquiring about my fainting spells, neurological episodes, or even my actual symptoms, he made small talk: *Where are you from? Do you have children? Why did you choose psychology*? (All lovely questions, if we were on a first date instead of a desperate search for medical answers.) The only piece of "medical advice" he offered? I needed more sleep. After that groundbreaking revelation, he informed me that since I was already seeing a neurologist 2½ hours away, I should just... continue doing that. And, just to drive home how deeply invested he was in my case, he casually wiped down his shoes with an antibiotic wipe... *while I was speaking.*

But the cherry on top? His final note: *"Hopefully, they will be able to address the mental health issues."* To say I was frustrated would be an understatement. I was exhausted—physically, emotionally, and mentally—fighting every single day just to function, only to have my symptoms brushed aside as a psychological problem. How many more doctors would it take before someone actually listened to me?

In July, I noticed something strange—after waking up from an episode, I was dragging my left leg a bit. I brushed it off, assuming I'd just fallen on it during an episode. No big deal, right?

Wrong.

The next day, I woke up from another episode, and this time, I couldn't feel or move my entire left side. *At all.* Terrifying doesn't even begin to describe it.

So, naturally, I made my way to my favorite place—the local hospital—where I was once again met with their signature top-tier care (yes, that *was* sarcasm you detected). Despite me clearly explaining that I couldn't move or feel my left side, the staff repeatedly asked me to lift my arm and leg, poked and prodded me, and then asked—over and over—*"Can you feel that?"*

"NO, I CANNOT feel anything. NO, I CANNOT move my leg. That's why I'm here!"

After running a CT scan and other tests, the results—shocker—came back *completely normal.*

And the grand medical conclusion?

> *"...seems the patient does have a history of alcoholism* (oh, here we go again) *versus Oliver Syndrome, here reporting left-sided weakness and numbness. We do not believe this is consistent with a stroke and suspect it may be some form of a migraine or other atypical condition. No defects corroborate with the left-sided weakness; it could be a vague form of Todd's paralysis, complex migraine, or potentially psychiatric in nature."*

Translation: *We have no idea what's going on, but we're going to suggest it's either a migraine, something vaguely neurological, or all in your head. Also, here's another unnecessary reference to alcohol just because.*

And just like that, they wished me luck and sent me on my way.

A month later, I found myself once again in my favorite spot—the hospital—after experiencing multiple episodes in a row, during which I stopped breathing and needed CPR more than once. As usual, all tests came back "normal," except for a blood pressure reading of 87/68 (but hey, no big deal, right?). So, after a quick pat on the back and some generic well wishes, I was sent home—because who needs to breathe, anyway?

Hospitals love to tell you to get help if your seizure lasts more than five minutes, or if your eyes roll back in your head. Funny, I've had episodes lasting up to an hour with my eyes showing nothing but whites, and yet I'm supposed to just ignore it. Clearly, I'm fine. Sure, I can't feel or move my left side, but hey, no biggie—I must be perfectly healthy, right? Yet somehow, everyone's too busy patting themselves on the back for their "fine" diagnosis to look any deeper. What happened to "do no harm"? Because it's starting to feel like doing nothing is the real harm here. I had been through more humiliating, frustrating, and downright infuriating moments than I could count. At this point, it felt like a never-ending comedy show—except I was the only one not laughing.

I switched to a new primary doctor, and she was a total game-changer! Right away, she fast-tracked referrals to both the neurologist and cardiologist at the facility. She ordered extensive blood work, leaving no stone unturned—even for the most unusual possibilities. But, most importantly, she actually *listened* and acknowledged everything I was going through. We discussed various possibilities together—she explained why she didn't think they were likely, but ran the tests anyway, just to be thorough. For the first time in a long while, I felt heard and validated. What a relief!

I saw a different neurologist who recommended another MRI, and this time, the results showed a *"4mm probable intrasellar Rathke's cleft cyst,"* but everything else looked normal. In my mind, this brain cyst could be the source of all my symptoms, right? Finally, an explanation! But the neurologist reassured me that these cysts are very common, don't typically cause symptoms, and rarely change in size. So, no need to worry. He also ordered another EEG, this time a brief one in the office. Can you guess what the results were? Yep, you guessed it—*everything looked normal.*

So, here I was—back to square one.

The neurologist also referred me for an EMG test to check for any nerve damage that could be causing the numbness in my left side. The results, however, didn't show anything that would explain the numbness in my left leg. But there was an unexpected surprise during the test—when I took off my shoes and socks, both of my feet were bright blue—like, Smurf blue! *Surprise!* Needless to say, this led to a referral to a vascular doctor.

I saw a vascular doctor who diagnosed me with Raynaud's disease. Apparently, it's a common condition with no known cause, and the treatment? Just keep your feet and hands warm. So, now I get to enjoy the delightful surprise of blue toes from time to time. Nothing like a little extra color in my life—who needs regular feet when you can have "Smurf" feet?

In November, I woke up from an episode after a pretty hard fall, unable to talk. Even though I tried to scream as loudly as I could, only air came out. When I was finally able to speak, I was stuttering and slurring so badly that it was hard to understand me. Given my past hospital experiences, and with another MRI already scheduled, I refused to go to the ER. Why go through that again, only to be told I'm perfectly healthy and sent home? I had the MRI done, this time of my neck. The results? "*Mid diffuse degenerative changes; central canal patent, neural foraminal narrowing (mild to severe from C3-C7).*" In simpler terms, there was something there, but it didn't explain my symptoms. In the end, I was referred back to the "expert" neurologist 2 ½ hours away.

I kept following up with the neurologist 2 ½ hours away, who remained insistent on the PNES/FND theory, and that CBT was the fix. Funny thing though—I had actually started therapy *before* these symptoms decided to show up and make themselves at home. And, I kept at it through the whole ordeal. But despite my best efforts, my symptoms weren't just sticking around—they were multiplying and bringing along some brand-new friends.

Interestingly, the psychologist that I'd been seeing for nearly a year by then was completely against the idea that my symptoms were psychological. He was firm in saying that CBT wasn't doing a thing for me, and even wrote a letter stating that and requesting additional treatment options for me. So, during one of my follow-up visits with the neurologist, I thought I'd ask the big question: *What other options do we have here?* His response? Crickets... I guess he wasn't feeling very chatty that day.

Let's hit the recap button, shall we? Before all this madness, I was living my best life—beach strolls, working like a champ. And now? Well, things have taken a *slightly* less glamorous turn. But hey, who needs options when stress and trauma are the magic culprit, right? Oh, the sweet irony of modern medicine.

Picture this: nine months of seizure episodes, leading to more concussions and sprains than a professional stunt double. I was falling like a clumsy character in a slapstick comedy. Breathing problems? Check. Eyes rolling into the back of my head like a spooky Halloween decoration? Oh, absolutely. Left leg and arm decided to go on vacation? You bet. Wheelchair rides became my new cardio routine. And let's not forget my feet, which thought it would be fun to show off their new "Smurf blue" hue. Oh, and speech problems—those showed up uninvited, too.

But wait, there's more! Despite this circus of symptoms, every single test came back with the same glowing review: "You're perfectly healthy!" The brain cyst? No big deal. Cervical issues? Eh, nothing to worry about. Nerve problems in my leg? Pfft, whatever. Blue feet? Who's even looking? And of course, everyone and their dog was convinced that stress and trauma were the root of it all, and a healthy dose of CBT would fix it all—because clearly, psychological therapy is the magic cure for losing the use of your leg. Never mind that the psychologist was waving a big "NOPE" flag.

It honestly sounds like a mental health commercial at this point...

Having seizures? No problem. Muscle weakness or paralysis? We've got you covered! Abnormal movements, tics, muscle spasms? We'll take care of it! Trouble walking, talking, or swallowing? Come on in for therapy. We'll fix it all with CBT... the cure-all (even though we still have no clue what FND actually is or how to properly understand it).

My primary doctor was absolutely fantastic through it all, doing everything in her power to get me a second opinion or a fresh set of eyes on my case. But, like a broken record, every specialist I saw would take one glance at the so-called "expert's" notes (yes, the neurologist 2 ½ hours away), nod knowingly, and then—surprise, surprise—refer me right back to him. It was like being stuck in a never-ending game of medical hot potato, except I was the potato, and no one actually wanted to deal with me.

That was it. No new insights, no real help—just a virtual pat on the back and a *"good luck with that."* I was absolutely crushed, teetering on the edge of giving up. My entire life had been flipped upside down, and it felt like no one even cared. My body had declared war on me, and I was losing every battle.

And when the so-called "experts" throw in the towel, who exactly are you supposed to turn to for medical guidance? WebMD? A Magic 8-Ball? Because at this point, they're about as helpful as the doctors have been.

And so the saga continued. But despite the absurdity of it all, I wasn't about to give up. Because if I've learned anything from this rollercoaster, it's that no one knows your body like you do. And I was determined to find someone who would listen—even if I had to drag them along for the ride. My journey wasn't about proving that I wasn't "crazy"—it was about standing up for myself, refusing to accept dismissiveness, and fighting for the quality of life I deserved.

I'm not just going to sit here and let this take over my life. Not without doing and trying everything I can! Nope, nosiree, not happening. So, what did I do? I turned to my trusty Google and YouTube University.

I scoured every nook and cranny, turned over every stone, and explored every corner in search of information on functional neurological disorder (FND) - the sneaky culprit that had completely upended my life and become my new archenemy. The whole "it's all in your head because of stress and trauma" explanation just didn't sit well with me. I needed something, *anything*, to help me make sense of this madness! But, to my dismay, there was a severe lack of research available, and what little I did find seemed like it belonged in a dusty old library, stuck in the outdated "stress and trauma" mindset.

I devoured article after article, combed through website after website, and binged video after video. Let's just say I may have been slightly obsessed with my quest for knowledge. But hey, all that digging paid off as the puzzle pieces began to fall into place, one by one.

I discovered that Functional Neurological Disorder (FND) is basically what happens when your brain and body start playing a game of telephone—and someone along the line drops the message, spills coffee on it, or shouts it into a wind tunnel. It's like having a nervous system that occasionally decides to freestyle its own version of reality, just to keep things interesting.

While diving headfirst into my research (armed with snacks, stubbornness, and way too many open browser tabs), I stumbled into online support groups and finally—finally—connected with others also living with FND. After months of being told that my symptoms were *"just stress"* or *"in my head,"* I can't even explain the relief of finding my glitchy soul tribe. It was like discovering the VIP lounge of misunderstood humans, and y'all... I belonged there.

In those support groups, I heard every kind of FND story you could imagine. For some, symptoms started after a virus or accident. Others pointed to trauma or stress. And some? They just woke up one day in the middle of a plot twist with no foreshadowing whatso-ever. Some people got a diagnosis quickly, while others wandered a medical maze for years. And almost everyone had a story about a dismissive doctor who waved them off like they were auditioning for a dramatic soap opera instead of fighting a very real neurological disorder.

I learned that FND has been around forever—since the days of Plato (who, by the way, would probably have a lot to say about our current healthcare system). Over time, it's worn a lot of hats: hysteria, conversion disorder, psychogenic illness... names that often came with stigma rather than support. But the truth is, FND doesn't play favorites. It can show up for anyone, at any age, from any background or corner of the world. It's like an uninvited guest that crashes your life and refuses to leave quietly.

I've also realized that living with FND is a full-time act of resilience. Some folks deal with symptoms every single day, others go through periods of calm followed by unexpected flare-ups. Some find relief with therapy, medication, or neuro rehab. For others, it's a daily dance of trial, error, and adjusting expectations. There's no one-size-fits-all roadmap—just a whole lot of creativity, patience, and fierce determination.

The people I've met on this journey? Absolute warriors. Even when we're misunderstood, dismissed, or straight-up ghosted by medical professionals and well-meaning loved ones, we keep pushing. We adapt. We research. We advocate. And we laugh—because if we didn't laugh, we might just scream into the void (and some of us already did that, too).

We may have glitchy wiring, but don't mistake that for weakness. Living with FND has taught me that strength doesn't always look like charging ahead at full speed. Sometimes it looks like resting. Sometimes it looks like setting boundaries. And sometimes, it looks like getting up for the fifth time after life knocks you down, because you're just that stubborn.

So where am I now, after all this chaos, confusion, and connection?

SYMPTOMS SHMYMPTOMS

LIFE GOES ON

Well, as you've probably gathered by now, the past few years have been a real rollercoaster—minus the fun part and with *way* more unexpected loops. But after what felt like a full-blown nationwide doctor tour (10 states, 40 vending machines, zero answers), I finally hit the jackpot. I now have a primary care doctor and a neurologist who not only listen but actually read the info I bring and treat me like a human, not a confused medical escape room.

And let me tell you, feeling heard? It seems like a billable luxury service.

It's been over two years since I was found unconscious, and since then, I've seen enough doctors and specialists to start my own medical-themed reality show.

I kept getting referred back to the same neurologist two and a half hours away—because, apparently, that's the official "*We don't know what to do with you*" protocol. I've come to the realization that when it comes to FND (or many unknown disorders), many doctors are flying blind with a GPS that's permanently stuck on "recalculating."

What's even more baffling is the lack of research—at least in the U.S. It's like everyone just kind of shrugged and moved on. Meanwhile, those of us living with FND are stuck in a never-ending game of medical musical chairs. But here's the twist: I'm done waiting for someone else to figure it out.

I've become my own best advocate. Armed with a very organized (and slightly aggressive) folder of FND research, I now walk into appointments ready for battle. Inside that folder: articles, psych evaluations, and a very polite letter from my therapist explaining that CBT, while lovely for some things, is about as effective for FND as a Band-Aid on a broken femur.

I ask doctors upfront: "*Are you familiar with FND? How well?*" If they're willing to listen, I dive into it with them. And when they're not? I plant seeds anyway. I've even started asking how to initiate a study—because if no one else is doing it, why not me?

Just for fun, I sometimes write out smart, logical questions I know will stump them. Not to be rude—just to get their gears turning. Who knows? Maybe I'll be the glitchy spark that inspires the next big FND breakthrough.

And here's a little nugget I wish more people knew: It turns out you *can* see FND through testing—*if* you know what to look for! It's not just a "diagnosis of exclusion" anymore. Thanks to some brilliant researchers who decided we weren't all faking it after all, we now know that FND can involve measurable differences in brain activity, metabolic function, and neural communication. In other words: science is finally catching up to what we've been trying to say all along—this is real, this is complex, and this is not just in our heads. And I plan to be right there cheering it on (and fact-checking the footnotes).

These days, my research continues. I'm still digging into the nervous system, connecting the dots, and trying anything that might lead to better answers—or at least better days. What started as a desperate search to prove I wasn't "crazy" became a mission to fight for a life that still holds joy, meaning, and connection. Because while my body might be unpredictable, my resilience? That's a constant.

Let's talk milestones.

It's officially been two years since I've had a fully "normal" day. My left leg? Still out of office. My speech? Some days I sound like me; other days, I'm communicating via high-stakes charades. And there are those non-speaking days where I'm basically a human emoji. The symptoms? Oh, they're still here—loud and proud (minus the stomach chaos, which my trusty supplements now handle like bouncers at a club).

But while my body's still doing its weird little interpretive dance, I've gotten really good at adapting. Adapting is my new superpower. Acceptance? That's the sidekick I didn't know I needed.

This might not be the "normal" I dreamed of, but it's my normal now—and I'm making it work.

For the longest time, I chased the idea of "fixing" everything. I waited for the magic moment when I'd wake up and feel like my old self. Spoiler alert: that day didn't come. And eventually, I had to ask the terrifying question: *What if this is it?*

At first, that felt like surrender. Like I was giving up.

But actually? Acceptance isn't giving up—it's a peace treaty. It's me and my body calling a truce. We're still not sending each other love letters, but we're figuring it out. I adapt. I pivot. I improvise. I find new ways to move through life—even if it's with a mobility aid and a whole lot of sarcasm.

And trust me, living this way requires creativity. From figuring out how to shuffle through my house like a caffeinated baby giraffe to inventing an entire gestural language when words won't cooperate, I've had to get weird and resourceful.

That's not to say I'm skipping through fields of flowers humming empowerment ballads every day. Some days, I'm ready to take on the world. Other days, I'm one stubbed toe away from an emotional detonation. And that's okay. Living with a glitchy body means I've had to give myself a whole lot of grace. I've had to redefine what strength looks like—not as pushing through at all costs, but knowing when to pause and rest.

I've learned that self-love isn't about adoring every part of myself—it's about choosing myself anyway.

Over and over again.

I may never have all the answers. I may never feel "cured." But I'm still here. Still standing. (Okay, sometimes sitting or leaning, but still here.) This version of me? She's strong. She's witty. She's got a backpack full of coping skills and a PhD in adapting to chaos.

And she's just getting started.

That's where the real journey begins — not in fixing what's broken, but in learning how to live beautifully, joyfully, and unapologetically in this body, exactly as it is. So, if you're ready, let's talk about what it really means to adapt, to embrace self-love, and to find laughter even in the most ridiculous moments. Because if there's one thing I've learned, it's that **life doesn't wait for you to be "healed" to be worth living**.

Onward we go.

Section 2: Adjust, Adapt, Amaze - The Art of Rolling With It

SURVIVING THE SPIN CYCLE OF LIFE

The human body is downright impressive — capable of all kinds of amazing feats, like healing itself, growing tiny humans, and somehow knowing exactly when it's time for tacos. But it's also wildly unpredictable. One minute it's your trusty sidekick, and the next it's pulling stunts like a rogue circus performer with zero regard for your comfort. When your body throws a tantrum, the question becomes: how do you deal with it without completely losing your mind?

It all starts with perception. Staying positive when life feels like a roller coaster designed by a particularly mischievous engineer isn't exactly easy. And let's be honest — there's nothing wrong with taking a little time to grieve the life you had before. Throw a pity party, send yourself a "Get Well Soon" card, maybe even award yourself "Best Dramatic Performance" for that shower cry scene. You've earned it.

But after the curtain falls on that emotional meltdown, there's a choice to make. You can stay stuck in the "*Why me?*" spiral, or you can start rewriting the script. And no, this isn't about slapping on a fake smile and pretending everything's sunshine and rainbows. It's about noticing the little victories, the weird silver linings, and the moments that make you laugh in spite of it all. Maybe your legs are on strike, but your upper body strength is about to rival a Marvel superhero. Maybe you had a brain fog day and forgot how doors work (hey, it happens to the best of us!), but at least your sense of humor is still sharp. And on those days when even laughter feels out of reach, sometimes just getting through the day is the biggest win of all.

Adapting to a new normal is a bit like becoming the MacGyver of your own life — solving problems with a combination of stubborn determination, duct tape, and questionable Amazon purchases. (Who knew a grabber tool could double as the ultimate snack retriever?) You'll try things that work, things that absolutely don't, and things that will make you question every life choice you've ever made. It's trial and error, but with more emphasis on the "error" part.

And the ridiculous moments? Oh, they're coming. You might accidentally wheel yourself into a display of canned beans at the grocery store (clean-up on aisle 5). You could find yourself explaining to your neighbor why you're stuck in your own mailbox (hypothetically speaking, of course... I hope!). Or maybe you'll have a full-on showdown with a rogue stair that simply refused to co-operate (been there, done that). But those moments? They become stories. And every time you retell them, you reclaim a little bit of joy from the chaos.

Of course, not every day is a comedy sketch. There are hard days — the kind that make you question whether you have anything left in the tank. On those days, it's all about self-compassion. Giving yourself grace when you can't do it all. Taking a nap. Canceling the plans. Letting yourself feel whatever you're feeling without judgment. And celebrating the tiny wins — because getting out of bed, brushing your teeth, or even just making it to the couch is sometimes a massive victory.

Self-care will look different now, and *that's okay*. Maybe it's trading in high-intensity workouts for gentle stretches in bed. Maybe it's five-minute dance parties where you wiggle like nobody's watching. Maybe it's snuggling under a weighted blanket and binging terrible reality TV without a shred of guilt. Whatever brings you joy — even a sliver of it — is worth celebrating.

This next part of the book is all about how to roll with the punches — sometimes literally. From finding humor in the absurdity to practicing self-compassion, it's about taking back your power in the face of uncertainty. You'll learn how to adapt with creativity, grieve what was while embracing what is, and maybe even laugh a little along the way. Because even when your body's the boss of mischief, your spirit can still run the show. And trust me — it's going to be one heck of a show!

FLIP THE SCRIPT: TURNING CHALLENGES INTO TRIUMPHS

"R eality is 10% what happens to you and 90% how your overthinking brain decides to interpret it."
— Inspired by Charles R. Swindoll, with a twist of chaos brain.

Perception is like that one friend who always has an opinion about everything—often an opinion that's completely uninvited. It has this sneaky way of turning a tiny inconvenience into a full-blown crisis, or making a mountain out of what's really just a small, somewhat inconvenient hill. It can transform a seemingly impossible situation into an opportunity for growth, or at least a chance to practice deep breathing and internal eye rolls. When you're dealing with a health crisis, or when life decides to drop a surprise plot twist on you, perception is like your own personal filter. It either lifts you up or leaves you trapped in a loop of *"Why me?"* and *"Seriously, again?"* So yes, perception is kind of a big deal.

Imagine that perception is a pair of sunglasses you never take off. Now, depending on the day, those lenses can either be tinted with frustration, sadness, or even good ol' fashioned doom and gloom. On those days, the world seems dark and every little thing feels like a catastrophe. You drop your keys and suddenly it feels like the universe is conspiring against you. But then, on a better day, maybe you swap out those shades for a pair that's all about hope and optimism. And voila, suddenly, that same world looks more manageable—maybe even a little sparkly.

But here's the kicker: Changing your perception doesn't mean you have to pretend everything is peachy when it's not. No one's asking you to pull a *"The world is great and I'm fine!"* performance every day (unless that's your thing, in which case, kudos). It's about adjusting how you react to reality. It's about choosing to see the light—even if that light's coming from a glow-in-the-dark sticker you stuck on your wall in a fit of optimism.

We all have an internal narrator in our heads—like a reality TV show narrator, but *way* more dramatic. When life hits you with a challenge, that narrator can go straight into doom and gloom mode. *"This is impossible,"* it whispers in a voice that sounds oddly like your mom when she's trying to teach you how to fold a fitted sheet. *"You'll never get better. Why even try?"* But, *plot twist*: that narrator is not an impartial observer. It's emotional, biased, and occasionally needs a good snack and a nap. The best part? *You can rewrite the script.* The narrator may be loud, but it's not in charge.

Think about it: when you have a flare-up of symptoms, your inner narrator might say, *"Ugh, I'm so weak. This is never going to end."* But what if you gently push back with, *"Hey, my body's telling me it needs a little rest today, and that's totally fine. Rest is part of healing, like a pizza is part of dinner (preferably with extra cheese)."* That small change in perspective might not solve all your problems, but it sure as heck makes you feel a lot less like a walking catastrophe.

Reframing is like mental jiu-jitsu. You take that negative thought and give it a gentle flip. It's like turning a bad day into a *"Let's go on an adventure!"* type of day—okay, maybe not an *adventure* per se (no one's asking you to climb Mount Everest), but at least a shift to, *"I can still find something to laugh about in all this."* And when you start reframing, your life becomes a whole lot more like a sitcom and a lot less like a soap opera. It doesn't change the plot, but it sure does make the scenes more entertaining.

Here are some classic scenarios that show just how powerful reframing can be:

- **Situation:** You miss out on a social event because of fatigue.

- **Negative Thought:** *"I'm such a disappointment. Everyone's probably talking about how unreliable I am."*

- **Reframe:** *"Taking care of myself is a form of self-care. The people who really matter will get it. And I'm still the life of the party in spirit!"* (Plus, you didn't have to wear pants—win!)

- **Situation:** You struggle to complete tasks that used to be easy-peasy.

- **Negative Thought:** *"I'm a failure. I can't get*

anything right."

- **Reframe:** *"I'm doing the best I can with what I have today. Adaptation is a skill, and I'm getting better at it. I'm like a superhero in training, minus the cape, because that would totally trip me up."*

- **Situation:** A medical test comes back with no clear answers.

- **Negative Thought:** *"This is it. I'll never get answers. I'm doomed to live in medical limbo forever."*

- **Reframe:** *"Another step forward! This is like a treasure hunt. Sure, it's slow, but I'm getting closer to the map. I'll get there—probably with a snack in hand, because, honestly, who does anything without snacks?"*

It might seem like a small shift in perspective, but it's like turning a dial on your mindset from *"Woe is me"* to *"Okay, what now?"* And, spoiler alert: that shift? It's a game changer. It turns you from a passive observer of your life to an active participant. You're not just letting life happen to you; you're shaping your experience, one reframe at a time.

Now, let's be real. Changing your perception isn't always easy. Some days, it'll feel impossible to think anything other than *"Why does everything suck?"* That's normal. Reframing is a practice, not a quick fix. On the tough days, the best you can do is say, *"Well, today was a disaster, but at least I'm still here to complain about it."* And you know what? Sometimes, that's enough.

Here are a few tools to help you get into the reframing habit, even when the universe is giving you all the wrong vibes:

1. **Gratitude Journaling:** Every day, jot down three things you're thankful for. They don't have to be monumental—maybe it's a good cup of coffee or the fact that you didn't step on a Lego. Focusing on gratitude helps retrain your brain to seek out the positives, no matter how small.

2. **Affirmations:** Think of them as mental push-ups. They might feel weird at first, but keep doing them and you'll start to see the benefits. *"I am resilient." "I am worthy of love." "I*

am doing my best." Write them down, say them out loud, and eventually, you'll start to believe them—especially when you add in dramatic hand gestures for emphasis.

3. **The "What If" Game:** Instead of letting your mind spiral into *"What if everything goes wrong?"*, try flipping it: *"What if everything goes right?"* It sounds silly, but suddenly, you're opening the door to all kinds of possibilities. It's like a mental plot twist that makes life a lot more interesting.

4. **Mindfulness:** When your mind is doing its best impression of a hamster on a wheel, pause for a second. Take a deep breath and notice what's around you. What can you hear? What can you see? Being present helps ground you in the moment and puts a stop to the mental merry-go-round.

5. **Perspective Shift Exercise:** If you wouldn't say the things you're thinking to a friend, why say them to yourself? Try to treat yourself with the same kindness and compassion you'd offer someone else. It's a game-changer.

The importance of perception is huge. It's the lens through which we view our world, and let's be honest—it makes all the difference. Whether it's a minor annoyance or a major challenge, perception can either leave you feeling defeated or empowered. When you learn to reframe, you start to look at life not as a series of roadblocks, but as opportunities for growth, learning, and maybe even a little laughter along the way.

So, here's the truth: Life isn't about avoiding the difficult moments. It's about how we choose to face them. You don't have to be perfect. You just have to keep going, keep reframing, and remember that it's okay to laugh at yourself when you trip over your own feet. In fact, it's encouraged.

And as we move forward into the next chapter, we'll dive into something that doesn't lend itself to reframing quite as easily—grief. When life takes something important from you, perception doesn't always help in the moment. Grief doesn't allow you to "just see the bright side," and sometimes, that's exactly what makes it so complicated. But understanding how to navigate grief can help you not only survive it, but grow from it. Let's dive into that next, shall we? Buckle up, because the next chapter's going to get real.

Chapter Takeaway:

Shifting your perception may sound simple in theory, but let's be real—it's easier said than done. Life doesn't always hand us the tools we need, and those negative thought patterns can be deeply ingrained, stubborn little beasts. There will be days when no amount of reframing or positive thinking can mask the weight of what you're going through. On those days, you might find yourself feeling frustrated, exhausted, or even defeated. And that's okay. Change takes time, and it's a gradual process. Don't expect to wake up one day and have everything magically fall into place. The key is to keep practicing, even when it feels like you're not making progress. Every small shift, every tiny victory, counts. And if you slip up or fall into a negative mindset? That's part of the journey too. Just remember: tomorrow is another chance to try again. **You don't have to get it perfect—you just have to keep going.**

SAYING GOODBYE TO NORMAL (WHATEVER THAT WAS)

"G*rief is like a really annoying houseguest — it shows up uninvited, eats all your snacks, and refuses to leave. Eventually, you learn to live with it... and maybe charge it rent." — Inspired by C.S. Lewis (who said, "No one ever told me that grief felt so like fear"), with a modern twist.*

If you've ever lost someone close to you, you already know that grief doesn't follow a neat five-step check-list that you can knock out over a long weekend. It's not a project to be completed or a feeling to be filed away. It's messy. It's wild. It shows up uninvited—at the worst possible times—and refuses to leave quietly. Grief is more like the ocean than a timeline: some days are peaceful and still, others leave you gasping for air, wondering how the heck you ended up face-down in the sand. And the more deeply you loved or were connected to what you lost, the more intense those waves tend to be.

But here's the thing people don't talk about enough: What if the person you're grieving isn't someone else—what if it's *you*?

When chronic illness or life-altering health changes crash into your world, they don't just shake up your routine—they fundamentally change your identity. Suddenly, the "you" you've known and loved—your energy, your independence, your go-to hobbies, your career, your spontaneity—starts to fade or disappear altogether. You're left staring in the mirror at a version of yourself that you don't recognize, and nobody warns you how hard that can hit. There are no sympathy cards for losing your former self. No casseroles. No phone calls checking in on how you're handling the loss of you.

But the grief is real. It's heavy. It's confusing. And it's incredibly lonely.

There's this bizarre in-between space you land in where your old life is out of reach, but your new one hasn't fully taken shape. You might still look the same on the outside—so people assume you're fine—but inside, you're grieving the loss of the person you used to be. The one who didn't have to plan their day around energy levels or pain flare-ups. The one who didn't think twice about stairs or whether they had enough stamina to shower and make a phone call in the same afternoon. You miss her. You mourn her.

And yes, like any other form of grief, it comes in waves—and often in stages. There's denial. Oh, the denial. *"This is temporary,"* you tell yourself. *"I just need to push through. I'll bounce back soon."* You cling to routines that no longer fit, force your body into doing things it's not ready for, and ignore the red flags because surrender feels like failure. But eventually, reality shows up and denial gets the boot.

Then comes anger. That raw, bubbling frustration aimed at anything and everything. At your body. At your doctors. At people who don't understand. At friends who say the wrong thing (or worse, nothing at all). At the healthy version of yourself who didn't fully appreciate what she had. It's okay to be angry. Anger, as exhausting as it is, reminds you that you care deeply about what you've lost.

Then there's bargaining. If I cut out gluten, dairy, sugar, red dye #5, and joy—maybe I'll get better. If I meditate long enough, pray hard enough, journal daily, and do every single thing the internet suggests, surely I'll go back to "normal." You make quiet deals with the universe like you're negotiating for your life—because in a way, you are. You just want some control back.

And then, inevitably, the sadness creeps in. Sometimes slowly, sometimes all at once. The full weight of what's been lost lands on you like a wet blanket. You mourn the dreams that feel distant now, the plans that keep getting delayed, the hobbies that no longer fit. You feel disconnected, not just from others, but from yourself. This stage is hard. It's heavy. But it's also necessary.

Eventually, there's acceptance. Not the cheery, *"Everything's great now!"* kind. This is the quieter, more grounded kind of acceptance. The kind that says, *"Okay, this is my reality now. I don't like it. I didn't choose it. But I'm learning to live with it."* It's the realization that while you may not go back to who you were, you still get to decide who you are going to be moving forward.

And let's be clear—this process isn't linear. You don't just check off each stage and level up to healing. One day you feel empowered and hopeful. The next you're crying over a photo from five years ago and yelling at a chair for being too heavy to move.

Guess what? That's normal. You're human. That's grief.

Some days, you'll feel strong—maybe even a little unstoppable. You'll think, *"Look at me, adapting like a pro."* Other days, you'll feel like you've been hit by a rogue wave, wondering if you've made any progress at all. The important thing to remember is: both types of days are part of healing. Both have value. Both mean you're still in the game.

So what can help in those moments? First, let yourself feel it. Don't shove the grief down or tell yourself to *"just be positive."* Grief is sacred. It's proof that something meaningful was lost. Sit with it. Cry if you need to. Write about it. Scream into a pillow. It's all valid.

Second, start getting curious about who you are now. The new you may not be able to run marathons or work long hours or stay out late, but maybe she's learned to slow down. To listen to her body. To set boundaries. To notice the little joys. Maybe this version of you has strength in places the old you didn't even know existed.

And third, know that grief doesn't mean the end of joy. It's possible—beautifully, painfully possible—to hold both sadness and gratitude in the same hands. To mourn what was while still celebrating what is. Your story isn't over. It's just taken a turn.

Yes, the old you was amazing—but so is the you who's still here. Still showing up. Still finding meaning. Still laughing, crying, adjusting, grieving, growing.

So go ahead—grieve your old life. Honor her. Miss her. Celebrate everything she was. And then, when you're ready, start getting to know the incredible, resilient, ever-evolving version of you that's rising up from the ashes. She might be different, but she is powerful, and she is worth loving.

Grief cracks you open, but it also clears space—space to rebuild, to reimagine, and to reconnect with yourself in ways you never thought possible. Once you've acknowledged what's been lost, you're left with an invitation: to stop searching for the old you and start nurturing the one who's still here. And that journey? It begins with self-love—not the fluffy, feel-good kind, but the raw, real, roll-up-your-sleeves kind. The kind that says, *"Even like this, I am still worthy."* Because after the storm of grief settles, the next step isn't just survival—it's learning how to truly love the person you are now.

Chapter Takeaway:

Grief isn't just reserved for the loss of others—it shows up when we lose pieces of ourselves too. Whether it's your health, your independence, or the life you thought you'd have, that loss is real, and it deserves to be felt. There's no timeline, no tidy stages, and no magic fix. But in allowing yourself to grieve, you also give yourself permission to heal. Some days you'll stand strong, other days you'll be holding on for dear life—but every wave you ride is proof that you're still here, still trying, still growing. And that's something to be proud of.

Love Yourself Like You Mean It

"Fall in love with yourself. At least you know your own red flags and still show up." — Inspired by Lizzo-level self-love brilliance.

Self-love. It's one of those phrases that gets tossed around like confetti at a New Year's Eve party. It's sparkly, it sounds nice, and everyone claims to know what it means—until it's your turn to actually do it. Then it gets a little murky. Is self-love journaling in the quiet of the night with soft candlelight flickering as you sip herbal tea, or whispering positive affirmations to your reflection in the bathroom mirror like you're giving yourself a pep talk before a big game? Is it treating yourself to that giant double chocolate brownie you've been eyeing, just because? Well, yes. And no.

Self-love is one of those catchphrases that sounds simple in theory but can be confusing in practice. It's kind of like when a relative says, *"Just be yourself!"* and you're left thinking, *"Cool, thanks, but how exactly does one 'be yourself' when your laundry is piling up and your to-do list is growing exponentially?"* Yeah, it's a bit like that.

So, let's clear this up once and for all: self-love is not a finish line you cross after you've perfected your skincare routine or after you've said your affirmations one hundred times. It's a relationship—with yourself. And, much like any other relationship, it's not all sunshine and rainbows. There are moments of awkwardness, the occasional breakdown in the cereal aisle, and maybe some angry sighs as you stare at your reflection wondering why you didn't just get that extra hour of sleep. But, just like any relationship, it's also full of joy, breakthroughs, quiet victories, and a whole lot of grace.

Self-love is not always soft and flowery. Sometimes it's gritty, uncomfortable, and downright hard. It means learning to sit with yourself in the silence when the weight of everything gets too heavy. It means resisting the urge to trash talk your body when it decides to go on strike. It's recognizing that your worth isn't tied to how much you can accomplish today, how "productive" you are, or how well you can hold it all together.

And here's the kicker: self-love is inconvenient. It means going to bed early while everyone else is out having fun and socializing. It means saying no without feeling the need to explain yourself to everyone. It's logging off social media when the comparison game starts playing in your mind like an endless loop. It's taking a moment to breathe when you feel like you're drowning in responsibilities, and it's allowing yourself to cry in your car while belting out 90s power ballads because, let's face it, sometimes that's what gets you through.

Here's how self-love shows up in everyday life:

- On bad days, it's about giving yourself permission to do less. Didn't fold the laundry, didn't answer texts, didn't solve world peace? That's okay—you're still enough.

- On good days, self-love means setting goals, gently pushing yourself, and acknowledging the small wins. Maybe no one else noticed, but you did. And that's enough.

- When your body changes—whether from illness, aging, or stress—self-love is about saying, *"Thanks for sticking with me, body. Let's keep going."* Not punishing or wishing your body looked like someone else's, but giving it credit for all it's done.

- When your mind starts spiraling, self-love is about hitting pause, taking a deep breath, and telling yourself, *"Not today, anxious thoughts. We're just going to be here for now."*

Here's the mind-blowing truth: You don't have to feel lovable to love yourself. Let me repeat that for the people in the back: You don't have to be glowing with confidence 24/7 to treat yourself with kindness. That's like only watering your plants when they're looking healthy and green. What about when they're drooping and looking a little sad? You don't ignore them then, do you? No. You water them. You give them a little TLC. Same goes for you. You don't have to wait until you're at your best to be kind to yourself. You are worthy of that kindness at your lowest points too.

Let's squash another misconception: Self-love is not about being selfish. It's not about ignoring others or thinking you're the center of the universe. It's about ensuring your own cup isn't empty before you try to pour into someone else's. If you're constantly running on fumes, criticizing yourself along the way, you can't give your best to others. You need to fill your own tank first.

Now, here's a little challenge for you: Start paying attention to how you talk to yourself. Would you say the things you're thinking to a friend? A child? Someone you love? If not, it's time to change the script. Speak to yourself with the same compassion you would offer a loved one. Celebrate your efforts, no matter how small. Look in the mirror and see a person who deserves kindness, regardless of what's going "right" or "wrong" in their life. You deserve to be seen, not just as a project or a list of flaws, but as a whole person who's doing their best.

And here's the thing: This journey of self-love isn't linear. You won't always feel like your own biggest cheerleader. Some days, self-love will feel like flossing your teeth—it's good for you, but it's a struggle to keep it consistent. That's okay. This isn't about perfection; it's about progress. Every time you show up for yourself—even in the smallest way—you're practicing love. Real, messy, powerful love.

So, what can you do to show yourself some love? Go ahead—take that nap, write in that journal, order the fries (because life is too short to count calories all the time), say no to the event that feels too overwhelming, go for that walk that clears your mind, delete that toxic app from your phone, or wear the outfit you love but have been too nervous to pull off. And yes, dance like nobody's watching (and if they are, who cares?).

Because you—yes, you, with all your quirks, your imperfections, your messiness—you are worth showing up for. You don't need to earn love. You already have it. It's built right into who you are.

And if you're not feeling it yet? That's okay too. You are still worthy of love. You don't have to earn it. You just have to keep reminding yourself: *"I matter. I am doing my best. And I am enough."*

Now, here's where things get really interesting: once you start embracing self-love, you begin to unlock a whole new level of superpower—the power of adaptation. Because self-love is the perfect setup for one of the most important skills in navigating life's twists and turns: the ability to adapt. And here's the kicker: you don't have to love every single thing that happens to you or even find joy in every challenge. But what self-love does is make you resilient. It gives you the strength to roll with the punches, the flexibility to shift when life throws curveballs, and the confidence to face whatever comes your way with a little more grace and a whole lot more self-compassion. So, buckle up, because adapting to your new normal isn't just a possibility—it can actually be kind of fun. Ready? Let's dive into how self-love sets the stage for adapting to life in all its messy, unpredictable glory.

Chapter Takeaway:

The biggest takeaway? Self-love isn't a destination — it's a practice. It's not reserved for your best days or when you feel like you "deserve" it. It's something you choose, even when it's hard, even when you don't feel particularly lovable, and especially when life feels messy. It's about showing up for yourself with compassion, giving yourself the same patience and care you'd offer a loved one, and remembering that you are worthy — right now, exactly as you are. So keep showing up, keep trying, and keep loving yourself through it all. You're doing better than you think.

ADAPTATION STATION - NEXT STOP, WHO KNOWS?

"*Adaptation is just evolution's way of saying, 'Plot twist!'" — Richard Dawkins' cool cousin who majored in improv*

Remember when we chatted about acceptance earlier — that fun little gem from the grief process? Well, once you've wrapped your head around the whole "*Okay, this is my life now*" part, it's time for the next step: adapting to your new normal.

Adapting is more than just surviving; it's about learning how to thrive in the face of change. Think of it like upgrading your phone's operating system. Sure, there's a learning curve at first. The new layout might drive you bonkers, some old apps might not work, and a few features might mysteriously disappear. But eventually, you figure it out, find new tricks, and maybe—even dare I say—the new version ends up being better than the old one. Adapting is about taking that "update" and making it work for you—quirks, glitches, and all.

Here's where perception really comes into play. It's way too easy to get stuck in the "*I can't do this anymore*" spiral. Trust me, I've been there. But a little mental shift can make a world of difference. Instead of thinking, "*I can't do X anymore*," flip it to, "*I CAN do Y... or maybe even X, just with a little remix.*" It's about finding new paths to your goals, even if they're not exactly the ones you expected. Life handed you a "challenge mode" version of your favorite activities—you just have to channel your inner MacGyver and get creative.

For example, maybe you loved long hikes, but now walking distances is a challenge. No trail adventure? Take a scenic drive instead, windows down, playlist blasting, and enjoy nature your way. Cooking? Enter the air fryer and slow cooker. Hot stoves, sharp knives, and unpredictable episodes meant I had to rethink my approach. Even on rough days, I can still whip up meals without turning my kitchen into a disaster zone.

Physical adaptations are key, too. My left leg may still be numb, but leg braces, walkers, and crutches have helped me regain movement. That first wobbly walk felt like discovering a new playground. I still rely on my wheelchair for safety, but I've learned to embrace whatever method helps me get through the day.

Speech, one-handed tasks, navigating the house—I've had to get creative with all of it. Apps that read aloud what I type, tongue twisters, stress balls, giant pens, helmets—you name it. Life has become a toolbox of adaptations. And humor? That's the glue holding it all together. Laughing at the ridiculousness keeps me moving forward when nothing else makes sense.

Ways to Adapt to Your "New Abnormal Normal"

Adapting isn't one-size-fits-all. Your "new normal" will likely look completely different from mine, and that's okay. The trick is to get curious about what works for you and be willing to try things—even if they feel a little silly at first. Here are some ideas to spark your creativity (and maybe a little laughter):

- Rethink your routines: Maybe mornings used to start with a full workout, hot shower, and green smoothie. Now? Yoga stretches in bed, lukewarm coffee, and letting your cat sit on your chest for emotional support. Accept it. Adapt it. Celebrate it.

- Hack your hobbies: Love painting but your hands cramp? Try watercolor pencils or digital art apps. Baking a cake feels impossible? Muffins in silicone cups might be your new jam. The goal isn't perfection—it's creative participation.

- Micro-wins matter: Can't go on long walks? Try mini strolls or backyard laps. Can't cook elaborate meals? Celebrate that you made toast without setting off the smoke alarm. Tiny victories build momentum.

- Tools are your friends: Walking aids, voice-to-text apps, adaptive utensils, sticky notes—these aren't cheats. They're magic wands for your "new abnormal normal."

- Social adaptations: Shorter meetups, virtual

hangouts, or funny voice notes instead of long calls. Participation counts, even if it looks different than before.

- Mindset gymnastics: "I can't do X the way I used to" → "I can do Y instead, and it might even be more fun." Mental MacGyvering: obstacles → opportunities.

- Celebrate your resilience: Every workaround, every laugh, every tiny victory deserves a high-five—maybe even a little dance. You're not just surviving; you're thriving in your own unique way.

Remember: adaptation isn't about comparison. Your "new normal" doesn't have to look like anyone else's. Apples and oranges, folks. You do you.

Chapter Takeaway:

The biggest takeaway? Adapting isn't about returning to who you were. It's about embracing who you are now and finding new ways to live fully, even in the face of change. Life's curveballs might throw off your plans, but with a little creativity, a willingness to rethink the familiar, and a good sense of humor, you can discover new paths to joy and purpose. Adapting is less about perfect solutions and more about making the most of what you have and rolling with the punches. Life might not be exactly what you expected, but with the right mindset, it can still be pretty great.

Keep Calm and Don't Take It Personally

"It's not about you. It's probably never been about you. Most people are just starring in their own chaotic soap opera." — Not Confucius, but he'd probably nod knowingly

If I had a dollar for every time someone said, *"Just think positively,"* or *"You're so strong,"* I'd probably have enough money to pay for all my therapy sessions. And let's be real, I'd be booking an entire week of them just to process how annoying those comments can be when you're deep in a health struggle. Don't get me wrong, I know people mean well. They're just trying to be supportive, but sometimes, those well-meaning phrases can feel like daggers when you're in the thick of things. It's hard to swallow advice like, *"Don't stress it,"* when the stress feels like it's suffocating you, and it's even harder to nod along when someone tells you to *"think positive"* as your world is spinning out of control.

When your life is flipped upside down, and you're struggling to keep your head above water, people's words can often hit like an unexpected punch. It's not like you asked for this life lesson, and frankly, the last thing you need is unsolicited advice, especially when it comes from someone who's never had to deal with what you're going through. But here's the thing — even though the advice might be annoying, it's often coming from a place of love and concern, not malice. And learning how to not take it personally? That's your secret weapon for staying sane when the world around you seems a little too eager to hand out "helpful" tips.

The "Think Positive" Trap

Ah, the classic *"Just think positive!"* comment. It's like the one-size-fits-all solution for every problem. The problem with this phrase? It oversimplifies what you're going through and puts pressure on you to be happy or optimistic when you're just trying to survive the next hour. People love to throw around positivity like it's a magic wand, hoping that it will somehow fix everything, but after dealing with health issues for a while, you start to realize that positivity isn't always the answer — it's just the shiny version of denial.

So, when someone tells you to *"Think positive,"* your first reaction might be to want to scream, *"I am thinking positive! But right now, being positive doesn't mean ignoring the reality that I'm struggling!"* And that's okay. You can be positive and still feel frustrated, sad, or overwhelmed. The trick is to acknowledge those feelings instead of stuffing them down because, believe me, they'll come back with a vengeance if you don't.

How to not take it personally:

Next time someone tells you to *"Think positive,"* try to remember that they don't know how hard it is to do that in your situation. It's likely coming from a place of hope, not judgment. And it's okay to politely respond, *"I'm doing my best, but some days are harder than others."* You don't owe anyone an explanation for how you're feeling, but giving them a little insight can help them understand that positivity isn't always a switch you can flick on.

The "You're So Strong" Statement

Here's another one. *"You're so strong."* Look, I get it. People are trying to remind you of your resilience, which is sweet. But it's not like you *chose* this! Sometimes, when you're in the middle of a crisis, sometimes "strong" feels like an unfair expectation. Some days, *strong* is simply getting out of bed. Some days, it's keeping a smile on your face when you really want to curl up and cry. And that's enough. You don't have to be strong all the time.

How to not take it personally:

Instead of seeing *"You're so strong"* as pressure, think of it as a recognition of how far you've come. Maybe it's not strength in the way you imagined it, but the fact that you're still here, still fighting, still trying — that's strength in itself. When someone says you're strong, thank them. But also remember, strength doesn't look the same every day. Sometimes it's just surviving, and that's more than enough.

"I Know How You Feel..."

Let's be real: when you're being vulnerable — sharing your story, your grief, your struggle — and someone chimes in with, *"I totally get it. I went through something similar,"* it can feel... off. Like, really? You stubbed your toe in 2009 and now you understand my entire healing journey? Interesting.

But before we jump to conclusions (or across the table), let's pause.

Most of the time, people aren't trying to hijack your pain or turn the conversation into a game of *Whose Trauma Is It Anyway?* They're just doing what humans do: trying to relate. Unfortunately, not everyone has the emotional finesse of a therapist or the timing of a seasoned talk show host. Sometimes, empathy shows up in mismatched socks and says the wrong thing at the wrong time — but it still showed up.

It's a weird balance. On one hand, their intention may be kindness. On the other, it feels like your story just got swept into someone else's flashback reel. That sting you feel? It's valid. But here's how to loosen its grip.

How Not to Take It Personally

Start by assuming good intent — even when their delivery lands like a flaming squirrel in a yoga class. Most people mean well. They're not trying to one-up your pain; they're just clumsily reaching for connection. When someone says, *"I know how you feel,"* they probably don't — not exactly. But they might know what a version of that feeling feels like. And that's the bridge we can choose to walk across instead of burning it down.

Remember: while experiences can be wildly different, the emotions they bring out — grief, fear, confusion, exhaustion — can feel surprisingly similar. But comparing your struggles to someone else's is like comparing apples to oranges... that are on fire... in a blender. It's just not fair (or useful) to anyone.

If a conversation starts slipping sideways, steer it gently. A simple, *"Thanks for sharing — this feels different for me,"* sets the boundary without a fight. You're not being rude; you're protecting your peace.

And sometimes? People just won't get it. That's not a reflection of your story's value — it's just their limit. Don't let their inability to meet you in your feelings make you doubt the depth of them.

When all else fails, laugh. Because awkward empathy deserves a slow clap and a sitcom laugh track. Humor won't fix everything, but it keeps you in the driver's seat of your own story.

When People Move On, But You're Still Struggling

This one hurts. You're stuck in the thick of it, but life around you keeps moving forward. Friends are going on vacations, posting pictures of their nights out, and you're left in the dust, feeling like everyone else is living their best life while you're stuck in a never-ending loop of doctor's appointments and medical setbacks. It's easy to feel like you're being left behind or that people don't care because they're not checking in as much. But here's the thing — it's not about you.

People have their own lives, and while you're navigating this difficult time, they're probably dealing with their own struggles. It doesn't mean they don't care about you. It just means they can't always be there in the way you need them to be.

How to not take it personally:

Instead of feeling hurt or abandoned, try to see the bigger picture. People are living their lives, just like you were before your health took a nosedive. It's not a reflection of how much they care about you, but rather how life continues, even when you're stuck in a challenging moment. And, if you feel like they've pulled away, communicate with them. Let them know how you're feeling, and don't assume they know exactly what you need. They might be waiting for you to reach out. And when you do, you'll be giving them the chance to show up for you in the way you need.

The "Have You Tried...?" Advice

Everyone seems to have an opinion on how you should be managing your health, from the latest diet trend to obscure holistic remedies that require you to chant in front of a candle at sunrise. The problem is, when you're already overwhelmed with your situation, the last thing you need is advice that makes you feel like you've missed some magical, secret solution. It's not that the advice isn't helpful; it's just that you've probably heard it a hundred times already, and you're too tired to pretend it's the first time you've heard it.

How to not take it personally:

The key here is remembering that people are genuinely trying to help, even if their suggestions don't resonate with you. Instead of snapping, take a deep breath and say, *"Thanks for the suggestion! I've tried a lot of things already, but I'm open to hearing anything new."* This lets the other person know you're appreciative of their care without shutting them down.

How to Shift Your Perspective

Here's the thing — you can't control what people say or how they behave, but you *can* control how you react. The goal isn't to stop feeling hurt or frustrated when someone's words rub you the wrong way. You're human, and those feelings are valid. But by shifting your perspective, you give yourself the freedom to not take it personally.

Here are a few strategies for making that shift:

- **Assume Good Intentions:** People are rarely trying to hurt you on purpose. When someone says something that stings, remember that they likely don't have all the facts or understand exactly what you're going through. They might just want to make you feel better, even if their words miss the mark.

- **Communicate Your Needs:** If you feel like someone isn't offering the kind of support you need, let them know. People can't read your mind, and sometimes, they don't know how to show up for you. Tell them what you need, whether it's a hug, a chat, or just some quiet time together.

- **Give Yourself Permission to Be Human:** It's okay to not have it all together. It's okay to feel frustrated, sad, or angry. You don't have to always be strong, and you don't always have to be happy. Be kind to yourself and acknowledge your feelings, without guilt or shame.

- **Take a Step Back:** When someone's words hit you the wrong way, pause for a moment. Try to step outside the situation and ask yourself,

"What's their story? Why might they be saying this?" This can help you see the comment from a different angle and take the emotional charge out of it.

- **Remember That Not Everything Is About You:** This one's a biggie. People's words, actions, and attitudes often say more about them than they do about you. Don't internalize things that aren't meant for you. If someone is being short with you, it might be because they're stressed, not because you've done something wrong.

After learning not to take things personally, you might find that laughter becomes your best ally in the chaos. It's easy to get bogged down by the weight of everything, but let's face it: humor is often the best way to survive the storm. Life can throw some pretty ridiculous curveballs, and while you can't control what happens, you can choose how you respond. Finding humor in even the darkest moments isn't about ignoring reality—it's about embracing it with a smile (or at least a smirk). And trust me, when you start laughing, it feels like you've just found the secret weapon for making it through the madness. So, let's talk about how laughter can light the way, even on the days that feel more like an obstacle course than a walk in the park.

Chapter Takeaway:

Life is full of people who will say things that get under your skin, no matter how well-intentioned they may be. The challenge isn't in preventing them from speaking, but in choosing how you react. When you stop taking things personally, you take back control of your emotions, your thoughts, and your peace of mind. It's a superpower that allows you to navigate difficult conversations with grace, humor, and resilience. Because in the end, the only thing you can truly control is how you respond. And trust me, that's the most freeing feeling of all.

Laughing Through the Wreckage

*"When you slip on a banana peel, people laugh at you. But when you **tell** people you slipped on a banana peel, it's your laugh. That's the difference between tragedy and comedy."* — *Nora Ephron*

Laughter has always been one of my best survival tools, and trust me, I've gotten pretty good at cracking myself up. It's like I've developed a sixth sense for finding the quirky side of life. Take my speech, for example. Because I talk slowly to dodge the stuttering and slurring fiasco, I've convinced myself that I'd make an excellent English tutor. Seriously, I pronounce every single syllable like I'm narrating a fancy audiobook. You'd think I was prepping for a British period drama, not just trying to order coffee. Honestly, I could probably read a cereal box and turn it into a linguistic masterpiece.

And then there's my talent for accidental word mash-ups. If there's one thing I'm known for, it's blending words together that absolutely should not be in the same sentence. Picture this: *"I need to re-laxify"* or *"Let's just un-jumble this situation."* My brain plays its own game of Mad Libs without asking for any input, and at this point, I'm just rolling with it. I should seriously consider starting my own dictionary — *The Official Guide to Gibberish by Yours Truly*. I mean, who needs the Oxford English Dictionary when you've got my one-of-a-kind vocabulary?

Now, let's talk about the bruises. They're practically a fashion statement at this point. I'm like a walking canvas for a slapdash art project, except instead of fine brushstrokes, it's just me bumping into walls and door frames. But you know what? I've embraced it. Every bruise is a new opportunity for an abstract masterpiece. Connect-the-dots, anyone? Maybe I'll even make a game of it. Sure, I'm not going to make a Van Gogh, but hey, I get an entertaining (and totally unique) design out of it.

And then there's my signature move — the shuffle. Sure, it's not exactly the graceful glide I used to do, but I've mastered the art of the "one-leg slide." You know, the kind of shuffle you do when you're auditioning for a zombie movie but can't decide if it's a drama or a comedy. Without my brace, I look like a character in a horror film, dragging my left leg behind me like it's got a mind of its own. When I'm feeling fancy — or when I'm desperately trying not to faceplant — I clutch onto walls and furniture like a toddler learning to walk. It's basically like a walking disaster movie. But it doesn't stop there! Sometimes I even throw in a backwards stroll, which, let me tell you, is less like Michael Jackson's moonwalk and more like a moon wobble. Add in the tremors, and it's a full-body interpretive dance. Naturally, I've earned the title "Slide Queen," and I'm honestly considering crowning myself.

The truth is, life doesn't always go as planned, but that doesn't mean we can't find some humor in the chaos. Sure, I could sit around and feel sorry for myself, but where's the fun in that? Laughter is an art — like a muscle that needs to be stretched, practiced, and sometimes just thrown into the deep end. The more you do it, the more you realize how often the universe is just begging you to laugh. It's not always easy, but once you get the hang of it, life becomes a lot less like a tragic drama and a lot more like a sitcom with a ridiculously over-the-top plotline. Think of it as "laughing instead of crying" or "faking it 'til you make it" — either way, you're winning. And hey, when life hands you lemons? Well, you might as well make a lemonade stand, throw in some sassy humor, and sell it with a smile.

Laughter, my friends, is not only the best medicine — it's practically a workout. Seriously, if laughter were an Olympic sport, I'd be competing for gold. I've discovered that laughing has more benefits than just making things more entertaining. You know that saying, *"Laughter is the best medicine"*? Well, it's not just a feel-good cliché. Turns out, it's scientifically backed.

First off, laughter reduces stress. When you crack up, your body releases endorphins, those wonderful chemicals that make you feel like a million bucks. It's like your own personal cheer squad on standby. And let's not forget about the physical benefits — laughing increases blood flow, improves circulation, and strengthens the immune system. It's like a mini workout for your heart, only without the sweat or the awkward gym selfies. But it gets even better: laughter actually burns calories. Yeah, you read that right. A hearty laugh can burn anywhere from 10 to 40 calories, depending on how hard you're laughing. So, go ahead, laugh yourself into a slimmer waistline — it's pretty much the easiest exercise routine ever. Plus, it's way more fun than running on a treadmill.

But beyond the physical perks, laughter is also an emotional game-changer. It's like a reset button for your brain. When life's throwing curveballs, laughter helps to reframe the situation and put it into perspective. Instead of getting bogged down by what you can't do, it helps you focus on what's still working, what's still hilarious, and what's still worth celebrating. It's like giving yourself permission to step outside the serious, heavy atmosphere of life and into a lighter, more joyful space.

Here's the thing: when you're dealing with health challenges, it can feel like the world is always on fast-forward while you're stuck in slow motion. But that doesn't mean you can't still find the humor in your situation — even if it's just laughing at how absurd things can get. Life's unpredictability becomes a source of comedy gold. You can either sit there feeling frustrated, or you can look at the way your body (and the universe) is playing tricks on you and just laugh at the sheer ridiculousness of it all.

That "one-leg slide" of mine? Well, I've made it a signature move, and you'd better believe I milk every funny moment. It's not always about perfection or elegance.

Sometimes, the messiest moments are the funniest. I've even caught myself laughing at the way I say certain words — the accidental mash-ups I make are straight-up comedy material. What's the harm in seeing the humor in my stumbles, my missteps, and my slow-mo zombie shuffle? It's way better than sulking in frustration.

The best part of laughter? It's contagious. When you find the humor in things, others around you start to see it too. It becomes this beautiful chain reaction where everyone's giggling together, and before you know it, you've turned what could've been a miserable situation into a comedic highlight reel. It's like being the star of your own quirky sitcom, with a never-ending supply of material.

And yes, while it might feel like life's throwing some serious punches, laughter gives you the resilience to roll with it. It's your secret weapon for enduring those tough times. So, when things get rough and you find yourself staring at another one of life's curveballs, remember this: the best way to handle it might just be to laugh your way through it. Not only will you lighten your own mood, but you might just burn a few calories while you're at it. And let's be honest, that's the kind of multitasking we all need.

In the end, laughter isn't just a coping mechanism — it's a survival tool. It's what keeps you grounded, keeps you from taking life too seriously, and reminds you that no matter what, the universe can't take away your sense of humor. So laugh at the chaos, laugh at the stumbles, laugh at the absurdity of it all. Because at the end of the day, laughter is the one thing that nobody can steal from you.

Finding Humor in Tough Situations

- **Give Your Mishaps Silly Nicknames:** Did you fall over in the kitchen? Call it *The Great Pancake Disaster of 2026*. Spilled your coffee? Welcome to *The Espresso Explosion Chronicles*. Naming your oopsies instantly makes them funnier and way less catastrophic.

- **Pretend You're in a Sitcom:** Imagine there's a laugh track every time something ridiculous happens. That weird wobble while using a walker? Cue the applause. Dropped the laundry basket on your foot? Cue the laugh track and slow-mo replay. Life suddenly feels like a scripted comedy rather than a tragedy.

- **Turn Frustrations Into Mini-Skits:** Act out your day's challenges as a short performance—monologues, dramatic hand gestures, or voice-over commentary. Example: narrate your own speech app struggle like it's an epic battle scene. You'll either laugh or feel like you deserve an Oscar.

- **Use Exaggeration to Your Advantage:** When things go wrong, blow it out of proportion in a funny way: "I may have only dropped one fork, but clearly this is the *end of civilization as we know it.*" Humor softens the sting of reality.

- **Make Silly Self-Comparisons:** Compare yourself to hilarious, random things: *"I'm wobbling across the living room like a baby giraffe on roller skates."* Visualization = instant giggles. Bonus points if you say it out loud.

Now that we've cracked a few jokes and had some laughs, it's time to get a little more serious — but in a gentle way. Humor is a wonderful coping tool, but it's only part of the equation. To truly weather the storm of life's challenges, we also need to practice self-compassion. It's easy to be our own worst critic, especially when things aren't going the way we imagined. But what if we treated ourselves with the same kindness, patience, and understanding that we'd show a close friend? Self-compassion isn't about letting ourselves off the hook, it's about recognizing that we are human, imperfect, and worthy of care. And just like laughter, it's a skill we can cultivate over time. So let's take a deep breath and dive into the art of being kinder to ourselves.

Chapter Takeaway:

Laughter is more than just a way to lighten the mood — it's a powerful tool for survival. In the face of life's challenges, especially health struggles, finding humor in the chaos can transform your perspective. It's not about pretending everything is okay, but about choosing to see the absurdity and laughter in the mess. Laughing at yourself, at the little mishaps, and even at the stumbles, is a reminder that life doesn't have to be taken so seriously. Beyond the emotional release, laughter has real physical benefits — it can reduce stress, boost your immune system, and yes, even burn a few calories. So, embrace your quirks, find the comedy in your situation, and remember: laughter isn't just the best medicine, it's the ultimate survival tool that no one can take from you.

The Art of Not Being Your Own Worst Critic

"If you talked to your friends the way you talk to yourself, they'd ghost you. Be nicer. You're stuck with you." — Basically your therapist... or RuPaul on a gentle day.

Ever notice how you're basically a licensed therapist for your friends? You've got that uncanny ability to dish out the best advice, offer a shoulder to cry on, and listen so intently that your ears practically deserve a gold star. You go out of your way to make sure others are okay, and when it comes to forgiving people — especially those you love — you're basically a saint. But then, when it comes to giving that same level of care to yourself, it's like you've forgotten how. You're handing out free passes to everyone, but when it comes to you? You're stuck in permanent "no mercy" mode.

Seriously, think about it: If your best friend were suddenly dealing with health issues, would you berate them for not being perfect, for having a bad day, or for not handling everything like a superhero? Of course not! You'd move mountains to help them find answers, support them through every challenge, and shower them with understanding and compassion. You'd tell them, *"Hey, take it easy. You're doing your best, and that's enough."* So, why not offer yourself the same kindness? Why does it feel so much harder to extend that same grace to ourselves?

The truth is, self-compassion is something we all need to practice more intentionally. It's easy to get caught up in the idea that we should always be strong, always be moving forward, and always have it together. But life doesn't work that way, especially when we're facing serious health challenges. Your life has changed, and that's okay. You're not the same person you were before everything shifted — and that's not a bad thing. In fact, it's a sign that you're evolving. Different doesn't mean worse; it just means you're in a process of learning, growing, and adapting to a new normal. And guess what? Learning always involves a little trial and error.

So why not give yourself permission to mess up? Mistakes don't define you — they're simply proof that you're trying. Think of it like this: if a toddler stumbles while learning to walk, we don't call them a failure; we cheer them on and encourage them to keep going. Why not extend that same attitude to yourself? If you drop the ball on something, miss a step, or have a rough day, it's okay. It's part of the process. Instead of criticizing yourself, try saying, *"Okay, that didn't go as planned, but I'm going to try again tomorrow."*

Take, for example, those days when everything feels overwhelming. Maybe you've been in a cycle of health issues, where your body feels like it's betraying you, or you've had to change the way you do things. It's easy to get frustrated or feel like you're not doing enough. But, let's flip the script. Instead of telling yourself, *"I should be further along,"* try saying, *"I'm doing the best I can right now, and that's enough."* It's about acknowledging where you are, without judgment or guilt.

And here's the kicker — self-compassion isn't just about feeling sorry for yourself or giving yourself a free pass to slack off. It's about recognizing your worth even when things aren't perfect. For example, when I have days where I can't get out of bed or I can't manage certain tasks, I've learned to be gentle with myself. I may not be able to check off every item on my to-do list, but I can celebrate the small victories, like getting a shower or managing a meal. That's progress too!

Why is self-compassion so important? Because it's what fuels resilience. When life gets tough and your health challenges start to feel like mountains, self-compassion helps you climb them with a sense of patience and kindness instead of self-criticism. It allows you to acknowledge your limitations without feeling defeated by them. Instead of being trapped in a cycle of shame and frustration, you start to believe that you are enough, exactly as you are, flaws and all.

Self-compassion is also crucial for mental health. When we practice it, we reduce the impact of stress and negativity. It's like giving your brain a break from the constant "shoulds" and "coulds" and simply allowing yourself to be human. Instead of punishing yourself for every slip-up, you show yourself kindness, understanding, and acceptance. This, in turn, creates a sense of inner peace and balance.

Let's take it a step further. Have you ever been in a situation where you were incredibly hard on yourself, but then you realized, *"Hey, if a friend came to me with this same issue, I'd tell them it's okay"*? Why do we do that? We extend grace to others, yet we rarely extend the same to ourselves. The key is to become your own best friend. So next time you're facing a challenge or a tough moment, try to treat yourself with the same compassion you would offer to someone you care about deeply.

Take it from me — there will be days when things don't go right. There will be times when you feel frustrated, when things don't work the way you planned, or when you feel like you're losing ground. But on those days, remind yourself: you are worthy of kindness, especially from yourself. Celebrate your progress, no matter how small, and give yourself the grace to be imperfect.

Self-compassion isn't about ignoring the challenges you're facing or pretending everything is fine. It's about embracing yourself in all your humanity, flaws and triumphs alike. It's knowing that you're not defined by the difficult moments, but by your ability to love and care for yourself through them. And that's what will ultimately give you the strength to keep going — one step, one breath, and one act of kindness at a time.

Now that we've gotten cozy with self-compassion, let's switch gears and talk about something even more exciting: celebrating the small wins! We all love a big victory — but let's be real, life doesn't always hand us giant trophies. So, why not throw a party for the little things? Those tiny moments, like managing to tie your shoes or making it through the day without a meltdown, are the unsung heroes of life. And guess what? They deserve confetti! In the next chapter, we're going to talk about how to stop waiting for the big "W" and start throwing confetti at the small, hilarious, and sometimes quirky wins. Because who says a mini victory can't feel as epic as a grand one? Let's pop some virtual champagne and celebrate everything you're crushing, one small win at a time!

Chapter Takeaway:

Self-compassion is not a luxury, it's a necessity. We often show more kindness and understanding to others than we do to ourselves, but the truth is, we deserve that same grace. Life changes, challenges arise, and we make mistakes — and that's okay. Embrace the journey of learning, growing, and adapting with patience and kindness. Instead of harsh self-criticism, offer yourself the same empathy, encouragement, and understanding you would give to a friend. You are enough, exactly as you are, and showing yourself compassion fuels resilience, reduces stress, and strengthens your mental and emotional health. So, be your own best friend, celebrate your small victories, and remember: you're doing your best — and that's more than enough.

EVERY STEP COUNTS—ESPECIALLY THE WOBBLY ONES

"Celebrate every tiny victory. Brushed your teeth? You're basically a rockstar. Got out of bed? Olympic-level effort." — Inspired by Brené Brown, with a sprinkle of 'I tried today' energy

We're creatures of habit, aren't we? We get up, brush our teeth, make coffee, scroll through our phones, and check off tasks — often without really thinking about it. It's so easy to fall into this routine and just go through the motions, especially when life feels overwhelming. But in this cycle, we often miss the small victories. The ones that don't come with fireworks, confetti, or standing ovations, but are just as important. Especially when we're caught in that sneaky spiral of *"look at all the things I can't do anymore,"* it can feel like the small wins get overlooked.

But here's the deal: adapting to a new normal — whatever that looks like — is *never* a straight path. It's more like a winding, bumpy road with questionable signage, the occasional traffic jam, and construction detours that seem to last forever. It's easy to get lost in the *"this isn't how things used to be"* mindset, but what if we took a moment to step back and look at how far we've come? What if we celebrated the little wins along the way, even if they don't come with dramatic music or a parade?

The truth is, progress is sneaky. It doesn't always come with a big "ta-da!" moment. Instead, it's often the quiet, everyday victories that slip by unnoticed. Like the first day you don't need a nap after taking a shower, or the time you make a meal without it being microwaved, or even remembering why you walked into the kitchen in the first place. These moments may not seem like much on the surface, but trust me — they count. Every little bit of progress is still *progress*, and that's worth recognizing.

In a world that constantly pushes us to achieve more, be more, and do more, we often forget that the little steps matter just as much as the big leaps. That's why celebrating those small victories is *so* important. Because in these tiny moments, you're telling yourself, *"I'm doing it. I'm still moving forward. I'm still here."*

Now, I get it — you might think, *"But it's just folding laundry,"* or, *"I only cooked a meal today."* And you might be tempted to dismiss those moments as insignificant. But what if I told you that these small, "mundane" tasks are actually markers of growth? Each time you get through the day with a sense of accomplishment, you're showing yourself that you have the strength to keep going. These small wins are what get you through the tough days, the ones that don't feel like you're making progress at all.

Here's the thing: you can't always control the big moments, but you *can* celebrate the small ones. And trust me, those little celebrations are just as important as the major milestones. Every time you pat yourself on the back, you're reinforcing the idea that even on the days when it feels like you're stuck, you're still moving forward.

Now let's talk about how you can celebrate those wins — because trust me, you deserve it. Celebrating doesn't have to be a big production, and it doesn't need to be expensive. It's the simple, quirky moments that can feel the most rewarding:

- **Snack Attack Celebration:** Managed to make it through a tough day without a meltdown? Time to grab your favorite snack. Whether it's chocolate-covered pretzels or unicorn-shaped gummies, treat yourself to something sweet and completely unnecessary.

- **Bubble Bath Bash:** There's nothing like a bath with an unreasonable amount of bubbles to make you feel like royalty. Light some candles, cue your guilty pleasure playlist, and pretend you're in a dramatic soap opera, completely deserving of this luxurious moment.

- **Dance It Out:** Hit play on your "I'm amazing" anthem and just dance. It doesn't matter if you look like a malfunctioning robot — every awkward move is a victory lap. Bonus points if you've got a signature move. (Personally, I'm all about the "flailing inflatable tube man" vibe.)

- **Nap Like a Champ:** Naps aren't just for toddlers. After a win — no matter how small —

indulge in a luxury recharge session. Cozy up with your favorite blanket and recharge your energy. No guilt allowed.

- **Selfie of Success:** Take a selfie with an over-the-top grin and a dramatic thumbs-up. Snap a pic of your hard-earned victory and show off that accomplishment. Bonus points for filters that scream, *"I did it!"*

- **Blanket Fort Extravaganza:** Who says blanket forts are just for kids? Celebrate your success by building a cozy, pillow-filled fortress. It's a chance to channel your inner architect and indulge in a guilty-pleasure binge-watch of your favorite feel-good show.

- **Victory Lap with Furry Friends:** Got a pet? Time to celebrate with a cuddle session! No pet? No problem. A rogue sock or a decorative pillow will do just fine. Celebrate the win by snuggling with anything soft and cuddly.

- **Treat Yo' Shelf:** Ever eye a book and think, *"I deserve that"*? Now's your chance to indulge. Buy that book, pair it with a delicious drink, and enjoy it in your fanciest mug. Because let's face it, *everything* tastes better in a fancy mug.

- **Plant Parent Power Move:** Add a new leafy friend to your plant collection. They'll stand tall like a little cheerleader, reminding you that growth (both literal and metaphorical) is always worth celebrating.

The beauty of celebrating small wins is that it doesn't require a big budget or a massive production. It's about taking a moment to honor your progress, even if it's just a tiny victory. Every time you stop and celebrate, you're saying, *"I am enough. I am moving forward. I am worthy of joy."* And let me tell you — those moments of self-recognition? They're *everything*.

As you keep celebrating, you'll begin to notice how much better you feel. You'll build momentum, boost your confidence, and maybe even start to see yourself as someone who can handle whatever comes your way. Because you *are* handling it. Even when it doesn't feel like it, every little victory adds up. And the more you celebrate, the more you'll realize how much you're capable of.

So, what's next? Now that you're a pro at recognizing and celebrating your progress, it's time to dive into self-care. We've talked about the importance of honoring your small wins, but let's face it — without the proper care, those wins don't feel as sweet. Self-care isn't just about pampering yourself every now and then; it's about making sure you're fueling your body, mind, and spirit so you can keep showing up for the people and things that matter most. It's time to dive into why taking care of yourself isn't just a luxury — it's a necessity.

Chapter Takeaway:

Celebrating small wins is about recognizing the progress you're making, even if it doesn't come with a parade. The little victories—whether it's surviving a tough day, making a meal, or simply getting through a task without needing a nap—are just as important as the big milestones. So, give yourself permission to celebrate the small stuff! Whether it's with a quirky snack, a dance party, or a victory lap with your pet, these moments remind you of how far you've come. **Every step forward is worth acknowledging, and embracing the little wins boosts your confidence and motivation to keep going. After all, progress is progress, no matter how small it seems.**

Self-Care Isn't Selfish, It's Survival

*T*o love oneself is the beginning of a lifelong romance — complete with naps, snacks, and do-not-disturb mode." — Oscar Wilde, probably, if he'd discovered fuzzy socks

Okay, deep breath... we made it to the self-care chapter! And here's the plot twist: every single chapter you've read so far has actually been a part of this one. Surprise! Grieving? Self-care. Perception shifts? Self-care. Learning to laugh at yourself, honor your wins, speak kindly to your inner hot mess? All. Self. Care.

See, self-care isn't just a chapter. It's the thread that's been quietly sewing together everything we've explored.

You've been building it the whole time—one brave moment, one vulnerable truth, one tiny victory at a time. So if you're feeling like you're just now getting to the "good stuff," take a moment and high-five yourself because, honey, you've been doing the good stuff all along.

Now, let's unpack it. And yes, there will be metaphors. And snacks. (Mentally. But if you have real snacks, even better.)

Let's talk about self-care—and no, I'm not talking about the "candlelit bubble bath with lo-fi beats and a side of Himalayan salt lamp" kind of self-care (although honestly, I love all of that and will defend it with my last bath bomb). I'm talking about real, soul-fueling, sometimes-gritty, often-unsexy self-care. The kind that doesn't always look good on Instagram but definitely makes your life better behind the scenes.

Self-care isn't a trend. It's not something reserved for Sundays or influencers with matching pajama sets and spotless kitchens. It's not a luxury. It's a non-negotiable. And if you've been waiting for a sign to take it seriously, here it is, in bold glitter font: ***YOU DESERVE TO BE TAKEN CARE OF.***

Real Talk: Self-Care Isn't Always Pretty (But It's Always Powerful)

Let's start by pulling off the glittery sticker and looking at the raw truth: self-care can be messy, weird, and deeply uncomfortable. Sometimes it means making a green smoothie. Other times, it means crying into a pizza while rewatching the same episode of your favorite comfort show for the 11th time. Both count.

Sometimes it's turning your phone off because your brain can't handle one more notification that starts with, *"Hey, quick question..."* Other times it's dragging yourself out of bed to do the hard thing—like setting boundaries or booking that appointment you've been avoiding since 2022. (We see you, dentist.)

You see, self-care isn't about perfection. It's about presence. It's about choosing to show up for yourself with the same care and compassion you'd give your best friend or your favorite pet. (And let's be honest—we're usually nicer to our pets than we are to ourselves.)

The Unsexy Magic of Boundaries

Want to know one of the ultimate forms of self-care? Two words: **Healthy boundaries.** Yep, the kind of boundaries that make people say, *"Oh, you've changed,"* and you smile and say, *"Thank you."* Setting boundaries can feel like trying to assemble IKEA furniture without instructions—awkward, confusing, and occasionally rage-inducing. But once they're in place? Chef's kiss.

Saying "no" when your plate is full is not selfish. It's strategic. It's called emotional budgeting, and honey, you only have so many spoons in a day. (Shout out to Spoon Theory!) Guard them like they're your last fries. Because you can't show up for anyone else if you're emotionally bankrupt. Boundaries protect your energy, your peace, and your future mental breakdown from being rescheduled.

Rest: The Forgotten Power Move

Rest isn't just important—it's vital. And yet, somehow, we treat it like a reward instead of a right. How many times have you said, *"I'll rest when I finish XYZ,"* and then XYZ turns into a 37-tab to-do list with sub-tasks and color codes? Spoiler alert: you are not a robot. You are a human being with a nervous system that needs a break. And naps? Naps are holy. They are tiny rebellions against burnout. They are protest naps, and you deserve them.

So the next time you feel guilt creeping in as you lie on the couch doing absolutely nothing, just remember: doing nothing is sometimes doing everything. Rest doesn't mean you're lazy—it means you're human.

Advocate Like a Boss

Let's talk about self-advocacy. AKA: speaking up for yourself, asking questions, and refusing to be gaslit into thinking you're "too sensitive" or "making it up." If your gut says something's off, it probably is. You know your body. You know your limits. You know when something needs attention—even if the world around you is trying to hand you a blanket of denial and say, *"Just relax."*

No, Susan, I will not "just relax." I will advocate for myself like I'm trying to win a Lifetime Achievement Award in Badassery. Whether it's with a healthcare provider, a boss, a friend, or even a well-meaning family member who doesn't quite get it—you have the right to speak up for your needs without apologizing for existing.

Move It or Groove It (Your Call)

Physical self-care doesn't require a gym membership or the coordination of a backup dancer. It just means moving your body in a way that feels good to *you*. That could mean stretching, dancing, walking, or aggressively cleaning your house to Beyoncé. It doesn't matter what it looks like—it matters how it feels.

So throw on your favorite playlist and have a private concert in your living room. No judgment here if your "workout" looks like aggressively stirring pasta to a beat. You moved your body? You win.

Emotional Self-Care: Feel the Feels

Here's your permission slip to feel all the things. Yes, even the ones you've been trying to stuff into a metaphorical junk drawer with the broken chargers and takeout menus. Emotional self-care is allowing yourself to feel angry, sad, excited, heartbroken, hopeful—sometimes all at once, like a chaotic smoothie of feelings.

Talk to a friend, cry into your sleeve, write your feelings down like you're submitting a letter to the universe. Whatever helps you process. Just remember: your emotions are not problems to fix. They're messengers. And ignoring them is like muting your smoke detector during a fire. Let yourself feel. And then let yourself heal.

Social Self-Care: Find Your People

Social self-care is all about curating your circle like your mental health depends on it—because it does. Spend time with the people who make you laugh so hard you snort. The ones who text you memes at 2 a.m. or send voice notes that start with *"Okay, so don't panic, but..."*

Whether it's a group chat that gives you life or a once-a-month coffee with someone who sees your soul, protect your people and protect your peace. And if you're someone who recharges with alone time? That counts, too. Silence is golden. Solitude is sacred. Social self-care isn't about how many people you have—it's about how safe you feel with the ones you do.

Practical Self-Care: The Unsung Hero

Let's not forget the unglamorous but wildly satisfying side of self-care: practical stuff. Like finally tackling that overflowing junk drawer, deleting 700 unread emails, or doing the laundry before it becomes a sentient being. It might not feel deep or profound, but these little things add up to a sense of calm and control.

Even something as simple as making your bed can change your whole vibe. It's not about aesthetics—it's about saying, *"Hey, I deserve to live in a space that doesn't look like a tornado married a sock monster."* **Go you.**

Let's tie it all together: Self-care isn't one thing. It's everything. It's every choice, every boundary, every *"I need help"* and every *"no, thank you"* that reminds you: I matter. I'm not a backup dancer in someone else's story. I'm the whole dang show.

You don't have to be polished to be powerful. You don't have to earn care to be worthy of it. Self-care isn't a reward for burning out—it's the practice that keeps you going.

Whether it looks like rest or laughter, spinach or Skittles, hard convos or solo dance breaks—it's all sacred. It's all valid. And it's all yours.

So here we are—the big moment. All the chapters before this one? They were leading here. Because grief, joy, perception, humor, love, compassion, the tiny wins—they're all part of your self-care toolbox. You've been collecting them like treasures, whether you realized it or not.

Now, in the next (and final!) chapter, we're going to pull it all together into something beautiful. Not perfect. Not polished. But deeply, unapologetically you.

Let's take all that you've learned—about loving yourself, adapting, laughing through the mess, and showing up anyway—and figure out how to carry it forward. No magic formula. Just real life, real you, and a whole lot of heart.

Ready? Let's put it all together.

Chapter Takeaway:

The truth is, self-care doesn't need to be earned. You don't have to cross off 17 to-dos or run a marathon to deserve a treat. You deserve to care for yourself simply because you exist. Self-care is a practice—not a reward. It's the way you show up for yourself, every single day. So, whether it's tackling the hard stuff like saying "no" or indulging in the fun stuff like a silly dance party, you are worthy of this care, without exception.

At the end of the day, self-care is about showing up for yourself—even on the messy days. Because, let's face it, life's not always going to be a flawless Instagram reel. But it is going to be a lot more fun, a lot more manageable, and a whole lot less overwhelming when you make yourself a priority. So go ahead—treat yourself like the rockstar you are. Whether it's with a bubble bath, a silly dance in the kitchen, or a nap that could rival Sleeping Beauty, you deserve it all.

Recipe for Resilience: A Dash of Everything

So here we are — the grand finale. The last chapter. The glittery, slightly tear-stained, peanut-butter-smudged (oh, don't forget the chocolate!) bow that ties this wild journey together.

If everything you've been through was a recipe, it'd be part soul food, part survival stew. You've stirred together perception shifts, grief, growth, fierce self-love, adaptation, messy-but-liberating self-compassion, hilarious detours, tiny-but-mighty victories, and a healthy serving of self-care. (And let's not forget the seasoning — lots of WTH moments, a sprinkle of sarcasm, a dash of glitter, and a few accidental fire alarms.)

This wasn't the life you planned — but it became the life you *owned*.

Let's rewind for a second. Remember when life threw you a curveball? Or maybe a dozen at once? A diagnosis, a slow unraveling, a relationship shift, a body that stopped cooperating, a mind that needed extra care — whatever it was, it changed everything. The floor dropped out, and for a moment (or longer), you didn't know who you were anymore.

But now, look at you.

You *did the work* — not the shiny Instagram kind, but the real, raw, soul-stretching kind. The work that doesn't come with a certificate or a round of applause. The kind that happens alone, in the quiet, in the doubt, in the *"I can't do this but I'm going to anyway"* moments.

It started with **perception** — learning to see life through a new lens. Not rose-colored glasses, but maybe ones that help you spot softness in the middle of the storm. You realized that how you see something shapes how you live through it. And you chose to see yourself not as broken, but as *becoming*. Not as behind, but as *bravely rebuilding*.

Then came the **grieving**. Not just for what was lost — but for the imagined future, for the expectations you didn't even realize you'd built, for the parts of you that had to be let go. You sat in that sorrow. You let yourself feel. You didn't rush it. You cried in parking lots, laughed while crying, raged at the ceiling, stared into space — and through it all, you honored what needed to be honored.

That grieving cracked open space for **self-love** — not the cute kind (though we love a good bubble bath and fuzzy socks), but the gritty, loyal, *"I've got you no matter what"* kind. The love that showed up for you when no one else could. The love that said, *"I see you trying. And I'm proud of you."*

And you **adapted**. Oh, did you ever. You figured out new ways to do old things. You made friends with change. You built routines around uncertainty. You pivoted, improvised, rewrote, and rebuilt. You probably had at least one dramatic breakdown along the way (which, to be clear, counts as cardio and character development). And yet, you rose.

You also stopped **taking it personally** — when people didn't get it, when your body acted like a rebellious teenager, when plans fell apart. You stopped blaming yourself for things you couldn't control. You stopped letting other people's confusion become your shame. You chose peace over people-pleasing. And you started protecting your energy like the precious resource it is.

Somewhere in there, you learned to **laugh** again. Even when things weren't funny. You turned awkward moments into stories. You found levity in the absurd. You cracked jokes that only made sense to you — and that was enough. Humor became your safety valve, your reminder that even in the middle of the mess, you were still *you*. Bold. Brilliant. Funny as hell.

And then came **self-compassion**. (She's quiet but powerful.) You stopped talking to yourself like a critic and started speaking like a friend. You gave yourself permission to be a work in progress. You dropped the perfection game. You replaced guilt with grace. You reminded yourself that progress doesn't always look like forward motion — sometimes it looks like stillness, softness, or simply *staying*.

You learned to **celebrate the small wins** — the often-invisible victories that no one else notices but matter so much. Like taking a shower. Like texting a friend back. Like asking for help. Like breathing through anxiety. Like showing up to your own life when it would've been easier to opt out. You stopped waiting for some big triumphant comeback and started cheering for every single step forward.

And let's talk about **self-care** — the real kind. Not just skincare routines (though bless them), but the kind that says: I deserve rest. I deserve support. I deserve to take up space. You advocated for your needs. You held your own hand. You honored your body, even when it frustrated you. You became someone who doesn't just survive... but tends to themselves with reverence.

So now what?

Now... you keep going.

You keep showing up — even if "showing up" today looks like mismatched socks and microwaved coffee. You keep honoring your truth, even when it's quiet. You keep laughing, keep crying, keep living with all the glorious messiness of a fully human life.

Because this — this strange, beautiful, imperfect reality — is *yours*. You are no longer just surviving it. You're *inhabiting* it. Loudly. Softly. Fiercely. Tenderly.

And maybe, just maybe... you're starting to fall in love with the version of you that exists *now*.

That's everything.

Because here's what's true: You've cried in bathroom stalls. You've had panic attacks at the grocery store. You've laughed until you couldn't breathe. You've texted *"I'm okay"* when you weren't. You've kept going, even when no one saw it. You've made it here — to this chapter — not by accident, but by choice.

You stopped asking for permission to live your truth.

You gave yourself back to yourself.

That's revolutionary.

So, again... now what?

Now you give yourself permission:

To take up space.

To say no without apologizing.

To feel everything, even the inconvenient emotions.

To rest when you're tired, not when you're "done."

To ask for help without guilt.

To believe, without shame, that you are doing your best — and that your best is enough.

You've already proven that you're resilient. Now it's time to practice being *gentle*. You've survived the storm. Now comes the part where you get to *nurture the garden* that grew in the wreckage.

Because this? **This is just the beginning.**

There are more wins ahead — quiet ones and loud ones. There's more laughter that hasn't escaped your lungs yet. There are people who haven't met you yet but are going to love you *exactly as you are*. There are sunrises, deep breaths, inside jokes, comfy clothes, and moments of peace still to come.

There is magic ahead — not because you need a miracle, but because you *are* one.

So here's to you:

To dancing in the kitchen.

To surviving what you never thought you could.

To thriving in ways that surprise even you.

To loving yourself out loud.

To writing new chapters with softness and sass.

To the version of you that is still unfolding — beautifully, bravely, and without apology.

You are not broken. You are not behind. You are not too late. **You are becoming.**

And the best part?

You're just getting started.

For the Curious, the Skeptical, and the Late-Night Googlers

This book is based on my real, lived experience - **not medical advice** (the official, very grown-up disclaimer lives at the front of the book). But if you're anything like me and tend to fall into the *"I'll just look up one thing..."* research spiral, here are a few reliable places to start if you'd like to learn more about the conditions I mention. (And yes - they're real. I promise. I'm living, occasionally wobbling proof. Apparently I don't do "ordinary" very well... I go straight for the one-in-a-million bonus package.)

Happy researching! **Each one, teach one!**

<u>Auto Brewery Syndrome (ABS)</u>

ABS Information & Research - https://www.auto brewery.org/

<u>Functional Neurological Disorder (FND)</u>

Not Defined By FND - https://www.notdefinedb yfnd.org/

FND Hope - https://fndhope.org/

FND Guide - https://neurosymptoms.org/

ABOUT THE AUTHOR

Nia Fenix is a writer, storyteller, and advocate for anyone navigating chronic illness, disability, or life's unpredictable curveballs. She's spent years navigating the unpredictable world of chronic illness, learning to find humor in chaos, strength in setbacks, and find joy even when life refuses to play fair. Through her experiences, Nia shows that while chronic illness or disability may change what life looks like, it doesn't change the value, creativity, or spirit of the person living it.

Her work isn't about sugarcoating reality—it's about embracing the "new normals," advocating for understanding, and inspiring others to live happy, meaningful, and fulfilling lives, no matter what obstacles appear. Whether she's chronicling quirky coping strategies, celebrating tiny wins, or turning frustrating moments into laugh-out-loud stories, Nia reminds readers that life can still be rich, bright, and full of possibility.

When she's not writing, Nia can be found experimenting with safe-but-delicious kitchen hacks, perfecting her dance-floor moves for solo living-room raves, or highlighting ways to advocate for herself and others in the world of chronic illness and disability. She believes in showing up for yourself, celebrating resilience, and finding humor in the chaos.

https://fenixcreativeworks.com/